D1209487

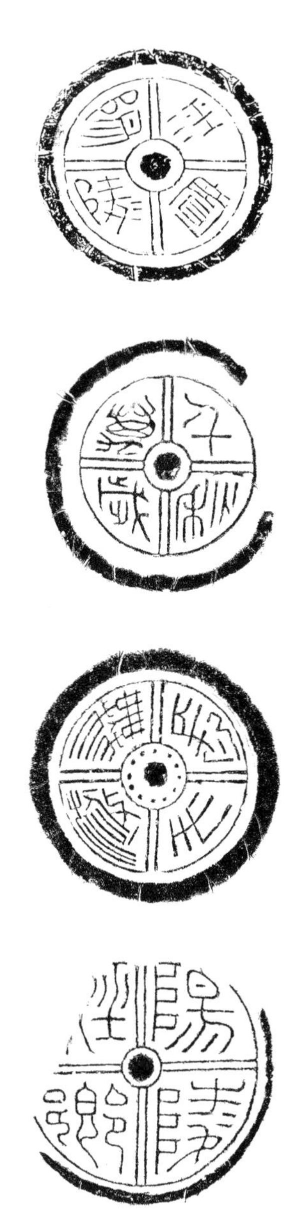

The Yangling Mausoleum of Emperor Jingdi of the Western Han Dynasty

陕西省考古研究所　编

重庆出版社

汉孝景皇帝刘启

汉阳陵

前言

九十年代以来，陕西省考古研究所对汉景帝阳陵进行了较大规模的考古调查、钻探和发掘，取得了许多令人瞩目的发掘研究成果。一九九九年九月三十日，以阳陵考古发掘研究成果为主要展出内容的阳陵考古陈列馆正式对国内外专家和游客开放。为尽快使专家学者们了解其概况，促进汉陵考古研究的进一步深入；同时也为了让广大游客充分领略“文景之治”的绝响神韵；在发掘简报即将刊行，考古报告紧张编写之际，我们特意提前编写了这部小小的图录，以飨读者。

一、阳陵的历史地理概况

汉景帝姓刘名启，是汉高祖刘邦之孙，汉文帝刘恒之子。他是继汉高祖刘邦、汉惠帝刘盈、汉文帝刘恒之后，西汉王朝的第四代皇帝。刘启生于汉惠帝七年（公元前188年），汉文帝后元七年（公元前157年）即位，时年三十二岁。汉景帝在位的十七年间，能顺应历史发展潮流，继承汉高祖、汉文帝所推崇的“黄老之术”，对内实行“无为而治”、“与民休息”，平定吴、楚、赵、胶西、济南、菑川、胶东等“七国之乱”；对外“和亲匈奴”；维护了国家的安定，加强了中央集权的统治，促进了经济的发展，使西汉王朝在汉文帝年间初步发展的基础上，达到了政治清明、国家安定、经济繁荣、百姓富足，形成了中国封建社会发展史上的第一个高峰。据《汉书·食货志》记载：“汉兴，接秦之弊，诸侯并起，民失作业，而大饥馑。凡米石五千，人相食，死者过半。……天下既定，民亡盖藏，自天子不能具醇驷，而将相或乘牛车。”到景帝末武帝初，西汉王朝则出现了“民人给家足，都鄙廪庾皆满，而府库余财。京师之钱累百钜万，贯朽而不可校。太仓之粟陈陈相因，充溢露积于外，腐败而不可食”的富庶景象。[1]因此，汉景帝及其父汉文帝被后世史学家称颂不已，所谓“汉兴，扫除烦苛，与民休息，至于孝文，加之以恭俭，孝景遵业，五六十载之间，至于移风易俗，黎民醇厚。周言成康，汉言文景，美矣！”[2]

阳陵是汉景帝和王皇后同茔异穴的合葬陵园。汉景帝前元四年（公元前153年）“更以弋阳为阳陵”，始作寿陵。“后元三年（公元前141年），甲子……帝崩于未央宫。二月癸酉，葬阳陵。”[3]“孝景王皇后，武帝母也。……后景帝十五岁，元朔三年（公元前126年）崩，合葬阳陵。”[4]

阳陵位于今陕西省咸阳市渭城区正阳镇张家湾、后沟村北的咸阳原上，地跨咸阳市渭城区、泾阳县、高陵县三县区。阳陵北濒泾水，南越渭河与汉长安城相望，东临“泾渭之会”，西与汉高祖长陵接壤。这里地势平缓，土厚水深，物产丰富，是古代人类较为理想的栖息地。加之其地近长安，控泾制渭，交通便利，因而也成为西汉帝王百年之后归宿的首选之地。西汉一朝共历十一代君主，除汉文帝霸陵、汉宣帝杜陵葬在长安东南外，汉高祖刘邦、汉惠帝刘盈、汉景帝刘启、汉武帝刘彻、汉昭帝刘弗陵、汉元帝刘奭、汉成帝刘骜、汉哀帝刘欣、汉平帝刘衎均葬在咸阳原上，而阳陵则是咸阳原西汉九陵中最东端的一座。

二、阳陵考古发掘研究历程

在现代科学意义上的中国考古学诞生之前，我国古代和近代就有许多历史学家、金石学家对包括阳陵在内的西汉帝陵具有浓厚的研究兴趣，他们或对帝陵的历史沿革、地理位置、形制规模加以记述和考据，或就帝陵出土的各类器物进行著录和考证。二十世纪初，日本学者伊东忠太、关野贞、足立喜六和法国汉学家沙畹、谢阁兰等先后对包括西汉帝陵、西汉长安城等西安附近的古代建筑、陵墓进行了初步的调查，其中1906年1月至1910年2月应聘为“陕西高等学堂教习”的足立喜六对西汉十一陵和西汉长安城进行了较为广泛的实地踏查和简略的勘测。1933年足立喜六根据其踏查、勘测和研究结果，由东洋文库出版了《长安史蹟の研究》一书。此书第五章“汉代の陵墓”中记载阳陵“茔域方千百七十方尺，方中四百八十方尺，陵高九十尺。”其测量和研究结果虽然十分简略且有不少错误之处，但仍可视为阳陵考古研究的开山之作。(5)

真正对阳陵进行现代考古学意义上的科学勘查是从本世纪七十年代开始的。1972年，陕西省历史博物馆的专家发现、试掘和确定了阳陵刑徒墓地；(6)1978年咸阳市博物馆的考古工作者对阳陵陵园进行了考古调查，勘测了帝陵、后陵、门阙、部分陪葬墓等；(7)80年代，中国社会科学院考古研究所的专家对阳陵进行了较全面的调查，取得了较大收获。(8)

一九九〇年五月至一九九四年十月，为配合西安——咸阳国际机场专用公路建设，陕西省考古研究所汉陵考古队开始对阳陵进行较大规模的考古发掘和研究工作。经过近五年的努力，先后钻探发现从葬坑两组、建筑遗址数座，并对其中的南区从葬坑进行了部分发掘。(9)南区从葬坑布局独特、内涵丰富、保存较好，出土陶俑等各类文物数量巨大，被评为一九九〇年全国十大考古发现之一。

一九九五年以来，新组建的阳陵考古队在以往工作的基础上重点对帝陵的结构布局及陪葬墓园进行了大规模地调查、测绘、钻探和发掘，进一步探明了陵园的整体布局和规模，大致掌握了帝陵的形制，发现了大量的陪葬墓园。同时还发掘了帝陵南阙门遗址，清理了一批中小型陪葬墓，发掘出土各类文物9300余件，取得了较重要的成果(10)。

一九九九年九月三十日，以阳陵考古发掘研究成果为主要展出内容的汉阳陵考古陈列馆正式建成并对国内外专家学者及游客开放，揭开了阳陵考古发掘、研究保护和开发建设的新篇章。

三、阳陵考古发掘纪要

通过发掘研究工作得知：阳陵陵园平面呈不规则葫芦形，东西长近六公里，南北宽一至三公里，面积约十二平方公里。由帝陵，后陵，南、北区从葬坑，刑徒墓地，陵庙等礼制建筑，陪葬墓及阳陵邑等部分组成。帝陵座西面东，居于陵园的中部偏西；后陵、南区从葬坑、北区从葬坑、一号建筑基址等距分布于帝陵四角；嫔妃陪葬墓区和罗经石遗址位于帝陵南北两侧，左右对称；刑徒墓地及三处建筑遗址在帝陵西侧，南北一字排列；陪葬墓园棋盘状分布于帝陵东侧的司马道两侧；阳陵邑则设置在陵园的东端。整个陵园以帝陵为中心，四角拱卫，南北对称，东西相连，布局规整，结构严谨，显示了唯我独尊的皇家意识和严格的等级观念。

阳陵帝陵陵园平面为正方形，边长417.5——418米。四边有夯土围墙，墙宽3.00——3.50米；四墙中部均有“三出”阙门，四角隅无角楼之类建筑基址。陵园中部为封土堆，呈覆斗形，上小底大，底部东边长167.5米、南边168.5米、西边167.5米、北边168.5米。封土顶部边长分别为：东63.5米、南56米、西63.5米、北56米。封土高32.28米。封土底部四边距围墙距离大致相等，约120米。

帝陵为“亚”字形，座西面东。墓室在封土下的中间部位，因封土堆积过厚，细部结构无法得知。帝陵东南西北各有一条墓道，墓道部分被封土所压，只有部分超出封土。超出封土的墓道平面均为梯形，内大外小。东墓道长69米、东端宽8米、西端宽32米，底部为13度的斜坡。南墓道长17米、南端宽3.5米、北端宽12米。西墓道长21米、西端宽5米、东端宽18米。北墓道长23.1米、北端宽1.8米、南端17.2米。墓道内均为五花夯土，土质较坚硬，土色红褐或黄褐，夯层及夯窝均不明显。墓道之上均有5——11米的汉代及其后代堆积。

帝陵的四条墓道探明之后，为了解有无多条墓道，我们沿封土底边的外围一周继续寻找，结果又在帝陵陵园四门以内，封土以外钻探发现从葬坑86座。其中东侧21座，南侧19座，西侧20座，北侧21座，东北角5座。东侧和西侧从葬坑均为东西向分布，南侧和北侧为南北向分布。四侧从葬坑与封土的距离除个别外，绝大多数为10米左右，其靠近封土的一端东西或南北形成一条直线，与封土底边平行。各坑间距最小是2米，最宽的为7米，一般均在4米左右。坑的宽度3——4米，绝大多数均在3.5米左右。最长的坑超过100米，最短的坑只有4米。坑深3米左右，坑底部距现地表8米，堆积层较厚的达14米。

帝陵东侧共有21座从葬坑，其中墓道以南11座；墓道以北10座，均为东西向，长度5——92米。从葬坑的西部边缘南北处于一条直线上，与封土底边平行。最长的13号坑东端距东墙仅26.1米。钻探资料表明，此组坑内有骑兵、步兵、动物等各式陶俑，陶、铜、漆器等生活用具及兵器、车马器等。帝陵北侧共发现21座从葬坑，其中墓道以东11座，墓道以西10座，均为南北向，长10——米。从葬坑的南端东西呈直线，与封土的北边大致平行。2号坑长95米，其北端距北墙22.6米。北侧坑内涵已知有各式兵器，车辆，步兵俑，生活用具等。帝陵西侧共有20座从葬坑，其中墓道以南9座，墓道以北11座，均为东西向。长度为5——100余米。20座从葬坑的东端除10号坑伸进帝陵封土以内，其余均与封土底边齐平。13号坑长100米，其西端距西墙26.5米。西侧的从葬坑内已知有骑兵、步兵、动物陶俑，陶、铜、漆器等生活用具及兵器、车马器等。帝陵南侧共有从葬坑19座，其中墓道以东10座，墓道以西9座。从葬坑均为东西向。最长的坑为27米，最短的坑为8米。南侧的从葬坑均较短，其南端距南墙91米。此组坑内的遗物尚不清楚。东北角的五座坑位于帝陵陵园东垣墙的西侧，呈南北一字形排列，其北端紧贴陵园北垣墙。此组坑内发现有朱砂、漆皮、板灰等遗迹和遗物。(11)

为了解已钻探发现的帝陵陵园86座从葬坑的形制及内涵，1998至1999年对帝陵东侧的13号、11号、19号等从葬坑进行了局部试掘。第13号坑为竖穴式长条形土圹，东西长92米，南北宽3米，深3米，坑底部距地表约8米。坑体为地下隧道式木结构框架。其构筑方法为：首先在原地面找平，然后逐层填土夯实加高约0.6——0.7米，再从夯土下挖约3米，穿过夯土、黑垆土、直入生土约1.7米。稍加平整后，在坑底部两侧铺上长条方木地袱，地袱上横铺木地板，地板之上的两侧有立柱，柱间镶有侧枋木，侧枋木上横铺棚木，棚木上部覆盖芦席，其棚木上部高度与坑口齐平，形成了一个隧道式的空间。随后放置陪葬品，最后用枋木封门。从葬坑的上部填有厚约3.5——6米五花夯土，夯层不太清晰，厚度为0.20——0.50米，较为坚硬。土色黄褐夹杂相当数量的红褐色土块。夯土之上为近代堆积层和耕土层。第11号坑长度为74米，19号坑长20米，其宽度、深度、结构、地层等均与13号坑相同或相近。

十三号坑上部棚木清理之后，露出了面向帝陵，排列密集的动物陶俑群，22米长的试掘方内按照动物陶塑的种类可分为四个区间。第一区间位于坑的东部，长约7米，均为彩绘陶山羊，共十九排，每排14件左右，共计235件。分黑色和橙红色两大类。山羊身长0.40米，高0.25米。其躯体肥壮，尾巴上扬，颔下有长长的胡须，神情温顺自然，造型生动逼真，雕塑工艺精湛。第二区间位于第一区间的西侧，长度亦约7米，放置彩绘陶狗28排，每排19——20件，共计458件。陶狗身长0.30米，高0.18米，有雌有雄。从物种上可分为狼狗和家狗两大类。从颜色可分为五种，即黄、白、黑、灰、橙红色，部分彩绘陶狗嘴唇和鼻子还涂有红色。狼狗竖耳怒目，长尾下垂。家犬短嘴小耳，尾巴上扬。陶狗均躯干粗短，丰满圆润。整体造型比例合度，模、塑、绘工艺精致，达到了形神兼备的程度。第三、第四区间在第二区间的西部，长度相当，均近8米。北半部为第三区间，出土六排33件彩绘陶绵羊，绵羊的颜色可分为黑色和橙红色两种，身长0.41米，高0.44米。双耳略垂，腿细长，臀肥大，细尾巴。造型栩栩如生，雕塑生动逼真。位于第三区间南侧的第四区间出土两排54头小乳猪。小乳猪长0.16米，高0.06米。分黑色和白色两种，乳猪竖耳、长嘴、小尾巴，生动逼真，憨态可掬。在此层动物之下尚有木板相隔，木板之下还有一层彩绘陶动物俑。因第一层动物俑未能提取，故不能进行下层清理，详情有待于进一步发掘清理。(12)

第11号坑试掘了其中部的24平方米，发现背靠帝陵面向东门的骑兵四列、木车两列，其中木车居中，骑兵分列两侧。发掘出土骑兵俑26件，彩绘木马17件，木车4辆，铜铁质兵器、车马器百余件。(13)

第19号坑试掘面积仅12平方米，出土木马4匹、木车1辆、武士俑20余件、动物俑10多件、铜铁质兵器、车马器及陶器等30余件。其排列顺序为木马在前，木车居中，武士俑两边护卫，动物俑及陶器等放置在车后两侧。[14]

此外，在第16号、第18号坑上部的盗洞中清理出“太官之印”、宦者俑等，为确定这些从葬坑的性质提供了重要的线索。[15]

阳陵帝陵南阙门遗址位于陵园南部正中，距帝陵封土120米，1997年3月至6月进行了发掘。共布10×10米的探方56个，实际清理面积3100平方米，发现大型建筑遗址一组两座，出土板瓦、筒瓦、瓦当、脊兽、围棋盘、博具盘、铁夯头等遗物583件。

南阙门遗址地面以上的地层堆积，大致可分为耕土层、现代回填层、汉以后堆积层和汉文化堆积层。遗址地面以下的地层堆积，为地面平整层、夯土基础层、黑垆土和生土层。南阙门遗址由一组两座三出阙相连接构成，三出阙的平面由大小依次递减的三个长方形组成。东西面阔131.5米，南北进深分别为25.4、17.4和11.0米。阙门的中间为中央门道，长25.5米，宽5.5米。门道的两侧为东、西，内、外四塾，平面为长方形，南北19.8米，东西10.7米。塾内地面铺有方砖。四塾的基础为夯筑，土质坚硬，土色黄褐。夯层厚8——12厘米，夯窝直径7——8厘米。塾外侧是主阙台，东西长27.5米，南北宽8.2米，残高6.21米。上部中间有东西向柱洞一列五个。主阙台外侧是副阙台，东西长14米，南北宽4.0米，残高0.4——4.3米。主、副阙台亦为夯土筑就，土质坚硬，土色红褐。夯层及夯窝同前。夯土外壁抹有厚约1——2厘米的草拌泥，其外先施白灰面，然后涂朱。塾、主阙台、副阙台周围环以回廊。回廊地面铺设方砖。南、北塾廊均长19.1米，宽1.5米。主阙廊南、北长均为31.1米，宽3.3米。南、北副阙廊长度均为18.6米，宽2.1米。回廊之外砌有鹅卵石散水，内高外低，呈鱼脊形。散水全长141.6米，宽0.9米。整个建筑布局规整，左右对称，结构合理，规模宏大，保存较好，是罕见的汉代建筑珍品。[16]

南阙门遗址的塾和主、副阙台，其基础夯土颜色明显不同，塾为黄褐色，主、副阙台呈红褐色，显然不是一次修建。在两部分夯土基础连接处，靠近主、副阙台的一侧施有草拌泥、白灰面和朱色，可见主、副阙台的年代略早，塾是稍后补建的。主、副阙台的年代应与阳陵的修建同期，亦即汉景帝年间。根据《汉书》的记载，汉武帝元鼎三年（公元前114年），“正月戊子，阳陵园火”。我们推测塾的补建时间，应在此次火灾之后不久。也就是说塾的补建年代为武帝年间。这一推测，与遗址柱洞中出土的五铢钱和早、晚两期的板瓦、筒瓦、瓦当等建筑材料不期而合。

阳陵后陵陵园平面亦为正方形，边长347.5——350米。四边亦有夯土围墙，四墙中部均有门，四角隅无角楼之类建筑基址。封土堆位于陵园中部，呈覆斗形，上小底大。后陵封土底边长度分别为：东157米、南167.5米、西156米、北151米；顶部各边长度，东61.5米、南48米、西64米、北52.5米。封土高26.49米。封土底边距各门距离均为110米。后陵型制亦为“亚”字形，座西面东。东南西北各有一条墓道，东侧墓道最长，最宽。封土外围亦有从葬坑。目前后陵钻探工作仍在继续进行。[17]

南区从葬坑位于帝陵东南、后陵正南。南区从葬坑范围东西320米，南北300米。共有从葬坑24条，长25——291米，宽多为4米。平面形状有长条形和“中”字形两类，均为南北向。24条从葬坑成东西向14行排列，每行坑数为1——6座，行距20米。其整体排列似有一定规律，即座西面东，南北对称。北区从葬坑位于帝陵西北，除座南面北外，其面积、坑数、行数、排列均同南区。90年——97年，先后对南区的14座坑进行了部分试掘或整体发掘，这些坑中有排列密集的武士俑群，有堆放粮食的仓库，还有牛、羊、猪、狗、鸡等陶质动物及成组的陶、铁、铜质生活用具，全面展现了汉代的军旅场景，可能与西汉当时的“南军”、“北军”有一定关系。[18]

罗经石遗址位于帝陵东南。此处地形隆起，外貌呈缓坡状。根据考古钻探得知，遗址平面近方形，边长约260米，外围有壕沟环绕。遗址中心部分的最高处放置着一块方形巨石，当地群众叫做“罗经石”。它用整块黑云母花岗岩雕凿而成，南北长183厘米，东西宽180厘米，厚40厘米。石板上部加工成直径140厘米的圆盘，表面刻有十字凹槽，槽宽、深2.3厘米左右，经测定为正南北方向。[19]据研究推测，它可能为修建阳陵时标定水平、测量高度和标示方位之用，是目前世界上发现的最早的古代测量标石。在对遗址的试掘中发现，遗址中部是一夯土台，应为主体建筑的台基。基址边长54米，共有12个门，每边三个门，四周有砖铺地面、卵石散水、四神空心砖以及瓦片堆积层等遗迹、遗物。这片建筑遗址地势高亢，布局规整，规模宏大，应该是阳陵陵园中最重要的礼制性建筑之一。[20]

刑徒墓地在景帝陵西北约1.5公里处。秦汉之际，帝王陵墓的修建工程主要由刑徒来修筑完成。据文献记载，秦始皇曾调集七十万刑徒修建其陵墓。《汉书·景帝纪》载：景帝曾“赦徒作阳陵者，死罪欲腐者，许之。”阳陵刑徒墓地在七十年代初被发现，其面积达8万平方米，估计葬于此地的刑徒在万人以上。72年发掘了其中的29座墓葬，发现了35具人骨架，其墓葬排列无序，尸骨凌乱，相互枕籍，埋葬草率，均无陪葬品。骨架上大多戴有“钳”、“釱”等类铁制刑具，有的还有明显的砍斫痕迹。[22]

帝陵陵园、后陵陵园的内部，帝陵的西部、北部，南区从葬坑的南部还发现有大量的建筑遗址，其详情有待于进一步钻探和发掘。

97年到98年，对位于阳陵陵园东部陪葬墓区进行了考古钻探和发掘清理，发现了规模巨大、数量众多、围沟完整、排列有序的陪葬墓园群。该墓园区西起帝陵东侧约1100米处，东到马家湾乡米家崖村塬边。全长2350米，南北宽1500米，总面积约3.5平方公里。其东、西各有南北向壕沟一条，作为陪葬墓葬区的东西界限。西侧壕沟已探明长440米，宽近8米，深6.2米。东侧壕沟长570余米，宽近40米，深约10米。中部有横贯陪葬墓区的东西向道路一条（司马道），西起帝陵陵园东阙门，向东直通阳陵邑。司马道南北宽110米，东西长3500米，路土厚0.1——0.24米，路土距地面0.70米。司马道的南北两侧排列有数量众多的陪葬墓园。墓园平面多为正方形，少数为长方形。墓园内有数量不等的墓葬和陪葬坑。墓园之间有壕沟分隔。目前已钻探发现东西向壕沟22条，南北向的壕沟百余条。及其由上述壕沟分隔而成的陪葬墓园16排107座。其中司马道南侧10排92座，北侧6排15座。这些墓园东西成排，南北成列，呈棋盘状分布。墓园内已探明了各类大中小型墓葬5000余座。对其中位于司马道南侧的部分古墓葬进行了清理。实际发掘古墓葬337座，其中汉墓280座，唐墓23座，宋、元、明、清墓34座，共出土各类文物5516件。在所发掘的280座汉墓中，包括竖穴土圹墓9座，竖穴土洞墓158座，斜坡墓道土洞墓77座，斜坡墓道竖穴土圹墓3座，竖穴墓道砖室墓11座，斜坡墓道砖室墓22座。汉墓中共出土各类文物5292件，其中有锺、钫、罐、仓、灶、鼎、钵等陶器1283件，以锺、钫、镜、带钩、车马器、弩机、印章、小铜饰等为主的铜器772件，半两、五铢、大泉五十、小泉直一等各类铜钱2923枚（组），铁剑、铁斧、铁灯、环首刀等铁器212件，玉圭、玉含、玉蝉、玉塞等小件玉器54件，骨、蚌、石、漆器等102件。

根据这些墓园的布局和墓葬型制以及出土遗物分析，上述墓园可划分为早、中、晚三期。

早期墓园已探明30座。其中司马道南侧2排，北侧2排。平面多为东西向长方形，有的近方形。大多无规整的门道，靠近司马道的一侧多无壕沟。有的墓园内有建筑遗址，个别的还有烧造建筑材料的陶窑。墓园面积4200——13000多平方米。发现东西向主壕沟8条，壕沟最宽为30米，一般宽度都在8——6米左右；深度一般为12.5米，最深达16米。壕沟断面为弧底槽形。底部有大量淤积土。壕沟内的堆积层中夹杂有汉代的粗绳纹瓦片等。一座墓园内有1至5座墓葬不等；主墓均为甲字形，墓旁一般都有从葬坑。司马道南侧墓园的主墓墓道多向北；司马道北侧的墓园主墓墓道多面南。在此区墓园中发掘清理汉墓60座，其中包括竖穴土圹墓2座，竖穴土洞墓35座，斜坡墓道土洞墓20座，斜坡墓道竖穴土圹墓2座，竖穴墓道砖室墓仅1座。出土陶、铜、铁、玉、骨器等各类文物1652件。其中在位于司马道南第一排的97YPIY$_9$——GYM$_{130}$出土的“周应”铜印一枚，经查阅《汉书》等有关史藉，证实汉景帝时有“周应”二人，一为西汉初年沅城侯周岩之子，景帝封其为郸侯，死后谥曰康侯；一为高景侯周成之孙，“孝景中元年，”以其祖成故绍封为绳侯。也就是说，97YPIY$_9$——GYM$_{130}$的墓主，若非郸侯周应，即为绳侯周应。[22]此外，在司马道南第一排97YPIY$_9$——GM144出土了锺、钫、盆等铜器数件，其中铜锺上刻有“般邑家铜锺容十斗重卅五斤第二家工造”铭文四行十七字。“般邑家”略同“阳信家”，应为某一诸侯或公主之封号。“般邑”（侯、公主），文献失载。M130和“般邑”的推定，结合史书有关丞相李蔡、苏建陪葬阳陵的记载，可以认为此期墓园的墓主都是诸侯、公主等皇亲国戚、朝廷显贵、郡国贵族。也就是说，此区墓园是阳陵的陪葬墓园。此期墓园特点是距离司马道近，墓园规模大、壕沟宽而深，墓形较大，排列有序，墓主级别较高。

中期墓园位于早期墓园的南北两侧，与早期墓园之间有约10米间隔。中期墓园55座。其中司马道南侧5排，北侧2排。布局较规整，排列较整齐。墓园平面多方形，边长在50——70米之间。墓园门道多向北方，宽5——25米。个别墓园内有建筑遗址，或有陶窑。东西向的主沟共有9条。墓园东西向壕沟东西笔直，明显是一次性测绘定位修建完成的，南北向的壕沟多数在一条直线上，但也有东西错位的现象。墓园壕沟较窄，宽度2.8——7.6米，多数宽2——4米，深度在3.2——6米之间。壕沟断面多数为平底槽形，少量为弧底槽形。沟内土质疏松，夹杂有汉代的铺地砖和绳纹瓦片，底部有淤积土。墓园内墓葬以小型和中型居多，多寡不一，最多的墓园内有百余座墓葬，最少的墓园亦有十几座墓葬。有的墓园墓葬排列似有规律，有的墓园墓葬方向不一，排列无序。墓葬类型多，有早晚打破关系。未见陪葬坑。在此区墓园中发掘清理汉墓120多座，其中包括竖穴土圹墓7座，竖穴土洞墓70多座，斜坡墓道土洞墓30多座，斜坡墓道竖穴土圹墓1座，砖室墓不到10座。出土陶、铜、铁、玉、骨器等各类文物1850多件。中期的墓园特点是距司马道较远，布局较规整，壕沟较窄，墓葬数量较多，型制多样，墓形变小，墓主级别较低。

晚期墓园位于中期墓园的南北两侧。与中期墓园之间有10米的间距相隔。晚期墓园共发现22座，其中司马道南侧3排，北侧2排。墓园平面方形、长方形，面积不等，还有大墓园内套小墓园的现象。多数边长在50——70米之间。门道方向不一，宽3米左右。晚期壕沟共有9条，总长度8491米。壕沟较前变窄、变浅。一般宽度在1.8——4米之间，深度在2.8——3.2米之间。壕沟断面平底槽形和弧底槽形。沟内堆积土疏松，底部有淤积土。墓园内墓葬较多，方向不一，排列规律不明显，有早晚打破关系。墓葬形制种类较多，砖室墓较前有所增加。在此区墓园中发掘清理汉墓近百座，其中包括竖穴土洞墓50余座，斜坡墓道土洞墓近30座，砖室墓22座。出土陶、铜、铁、玉、骨器等各类文物近1800件。与早、中期相比，晚期墓园距司马道最远，布局较规整，壕沟窄浅，墓葬数量较多，排列欠规整，墓主级别较低。

从文献记载、墓园位置、墓葬型制和出土器物分析，汉阳陵陪葬墓园时代上限应为景帝年间，亦即西汉早期，其下限到东汉中期。早期墓园的时代大致相当于汉景帝始建阳陵到汉武帝年间，中期墓园内的年代应在西汉中、晚期：晚期墓园的年代应从西汉晚期到东汉中期。早期的墓园应为阳陵陪葬墓园无疑。西汉中、晚期，许多皇亲国戚、朝廷重臣都陪葬茂陵、杜陵、平陵等当时在位的皇帝陵园附近，阳陵虽然可能还有陪葬，但部分墓园应是不以陪葬阳陵为目的的家族墓地。到了西汉晚期以后，陪葬阳陵已无必要，独立的家族墓地可能是墓园的主体。[23]

四、阳陵发掘的考古学意义

陵园整体布局的大致了解和掌握是阳陵考古发掘工作的第一点收获。三十年来，考古工作者对西汉十一陵的陵园、帝陵、陪葬墓、从葬坑、建筑遗址等进行了多次的调查、测绘乃至试掘，通过这些调查、测绘和试掘，特别是近年来阳陵的发掘和研究，西汉帝陵制度的神秘面纱已经揭开，西汉十一陵的形制特点逐渐明晰。

阳陵帝陵、后陵的钻探，发现帝陵、后陵均为“亚”字形，座西面东。帝陵东、南、西、北各有一条墓道，东墓道最长最宽，是主墓道。阳陵“亚”字形大墓和座西面东方向的探明，在西汉十一陵考古中是第一次。这次的发现基本解决了学术界关于汉陵面南还是面东这一长期争论不休的难题，否定了汉代帝陵依照昭穆制度进行布局的论点，解决了汉代帝陵制度研究的一大难题。[24]

阳陵陵园以内，封土四周钻探发现的86座从葬坑，排列密集，整齐划一。其内涵在钻探试掘过程中已有部分了解，有仪仗骑兵、武士和各类战车；还有兵器、车马器、生产工具、生活用具、食品库等，种类齐全、数量极多。在此之前，长陵、灞陵、安陵、阳陵、茂陵、杜陵等都发现过数量不等的从葬坑，但均位于帝、后陵园以外。这次的发现为汉陵的田野调查、钻探和发掘提出了新的课题，为帝陵制度的研究开辟了新的视野。由于这些从葬坑的分布和坑内陪葬物品的放置，无疑是按照当时宫廷的有关制度和需求埋藏的。因而对这批从葬坑的发掘和研究，对研究汉代宫廷制度、帝王生活、陪葬习俗都具有重大价值。

这次发现的阳陵陪葬墓园数量众多，围沟完整，布局规整，排列有序，显然是经过精心设计和安排的。这一现象暗示出西汉十一座帝陵陪葬墓区的布局和形制有可能均与阳陵相同或相近。历史文献中多有西汉皇帝赐大臣"冢茔"、"冢地"，以及"诸侯园"等记载，但因语焉不详，学者们一直不明究里，阳陵陪葬墓园的发现则对其作了简明的诠释，为汉陵陪葬制度的研究提供了不可多得的资料和线索。

以阳陵考古发掘资料为基础，结合其它西汉十陵的发掘研究成果，可以确定与商周时期的"集中公墓制"不同，西汉帝陵继承了秦始皇陵的布局结构而又有所发展，完成了"陵园独立化、陵园规模化、设施复杂化、功能完善化"的重大变革，形成了一种新的、与西汉社会制度相适应的"独立陵园制"，"奠定了而后中国近两千年专制社会帝王陵园制度的基础"。[25]

初步概括西汉帝陵的形制特点如下：1、西汉诸陵除霸陵依山为陵，是一种"因山为藏"的崖墓外，其余的封土均系夯筑而成。封土平面方形，多为覆斗状，个别陵呈二层台式；陵顶无"享堂"类建筑遗址。2、帝陵为亚字形，座西面东，东、南、西、北四条墓道以东墓道为主道。3、帝、后实行"同茔异穴"的合葬制，帝陵居中，后陵多在其东北；帝陵较大，后陵略小。4、西汉前期，帝、后陵居同一个陵园，一般为长方形，面积较大。阳陵以后，帝后各置陵园，间距一般在450——700米之间。平面方形，帝陵陵园边长400米左右，后陵陵园边长约350米。陵园四周筑以夯墙，每面垣墙中央各辟一门。阳陵帝陵四门为三出阙式，杜陵四门为两出台式。5、帝陵、后陵陵园的封土与垣墙之间有大量的从葬坑；帝、后陵园的外围也分布有数量不等的从葬坑。6、陵区内均有陵庙、寝殿、便殿等礼制建筑，寝殿和便殿一般在陵园内或陵园附近。7、西汉早中期诸帝陵均置陵邑，一般在帝陵的东或北侧，汉元帝时罢置陵邑。8、陪葬墓在历史上出现很早，而规模之大，首推西汉。西汉诸陵陪葬墓一般分为两个区，多数在陵东司马道的南北两侧，东西成排，南北成列，其间有壕沟分隔。个别嫔妃和身份特殊的居帝陵的北侧和南侧。陪葬墓根据级别或其他原因，墓冢外形分覆斗形、馒头形和山形。馒头形较多，覆斗形次之，山形最少。陪葬墓周围或有壕沟环绕，墓园平面多为正方形，少数为长方形，墓园内有各种建筑遗迹，如园邑或祠室等，大型的陪葬墓周围也有数量不等的祔葬墓和陪葬坑。9、大多数的汉陵附近都应有大片的刑徒墓地。阳陵的刑徒墓地位于帝陵西北约1500米处，其间有壕沟隔断。[26]

帝陵陵园南门三出阙的发掘和出土是阳陵考古发掘的第二大收获。阙是中国古代一种重要的建筑类型，在高等级、高规格建筑物如都城、宫室、陵墓等的大门之外或大门之处，多有设置。《释名·释宫室》云："阙，阙也；在门两旁，中央阙然为道也。"是为阙名之由来。阙的功能用途简单言之有四：A．观望、守卫。《说文·门部》"阙者，门观也。"《古今注》"阙，观也。古者每门树两观于其前，所以标表宫门也。其上可居，登之则可远观。"汉杨雄《卫尉箴》："阙为城卫，以待暴卒。国有以固，民有以内。"B．区别等级、尊卑。东汉班固《白虎通义》云："门必有阙者何？阙者，所以饰门，别尊卑也。"C．张示政令，听穷者冤。汉刘熙《释名·释宫室》："门阙，天子号令、赏罚所由出也。"《周礼·天官太宰》曰："象魏，秋天也"，"乃悬治法于象魏"。梁陆舺，《石阙铭》"以为象阙之制，其来以远，……或听穷者冤"。D、思过反省。《古今注》"人臣将朝，至此则思其所阙多少，故谓之阙。"上述第一点是阙的本来用途，也是其出现和产生的原因，而后三点则是其发展引申之义。《汉书霍光传》"太夫人显改光时所自造茔制而侈大之，起三出阙。"的记载证实上述的第二点到西汉以后形成一种阙的使用制度。即："一般官僚可用一对单阙。诸侯、二千石以上用一对二出阙，由一主阙，一子阙构成。""皇帝则用三出阙，由一主阙与二子阙构成。"[27]有专家认为夏商时期就出现了阙，可目前尚无确切的实物和文献证明。[28]《诗经》："挑兮达兮，在城阙兮。"和《左传·庄公二十一年》"郑伯享王于阙西辟。"《竹书记年》"鲁筑茅阙门"等的记载，证实至少在西周时期，阙作为一种建筑形式已经出现，但亦无实物留存至今。春秋战国以降，阙的记载更是连篇累牍、不绝于书。此前，考古工作发现的有关阙的图案资料有东汉画像石、画像砖，敦煌的壁画，唐墓壁画等；实物资料则有四川、山东、河南等省现存的东汉石阙以及新近发掘的唐乾陵乳峰三出阙、宋陵三出阙等。然而究其时代之早，等级之高，规模之大，无疑当数汉景帝阳陵帝陵南阙门遗址。因此，其发掘对门阙的起源、发展，门阙制度的形成、影响，以及中国古代建筑史的研究等有着重要作用。[29]此外，南阙门遗址还出土有目前发现最早的围棋盘（砖质）、陶质脊兽和最大的板瓦（残长108、宽43.5厘米）。[30]

数量众多、种类丰富的阳陵陶塑的大批出土是阳陵考古发掘的又一重大收获。截止目前，阳陵已发掘出土铜、铁、金、玉、石、陶、漆、木、骨、蚌、丝、麻各类器物及麦、粟、菽、黍等各类粮食标本等文物近五万件，其中数量最多、最具特色的是包括各类陶俑和陶塑动物在内的陶塑制品。

由于阳陵陶俑大部分为所谓的裸体俑，所以这些陶俑的身份、地位亦即其类型难以确定，但就其制作工艺、出土的位置、携带或附着的物品、身着的衣物及陶俑的形态姿势等分析，阳陵陶俑种类是十分丰富的。

根据其制作工艺的不同，阳陵陶俑可分为着衣式[31]（即裸体俑）和塑衣式两大类。着衣式陶俑出土于帝陵从葬坑、南区从葬坑和个别大型陪葬墓的从葬坑内。塑衣式陶俑多在一号建筑遗址和大中型陪葬墓中出土。结合近年来汉惠帝安陵、武帝茂陵、宣帝杜陵附近及汉长安城的制陶作坊等处考古发现，可以初步确定当时这种陶躯木臂，赋彩著衣的着衣式陶俑可能是专为皇室随葬的级别较高的陪葬品。而一般的贵族大臣在未经皇帝特赐的情况下不得使用此类陶俑，只能陪葬带陶塑服饰的“塑衣式”彩绘俑。

根据性别分类，阳陵陶俑的性别除了男性和女性外，还发现了宦者俑。[32]在秦始皇陵长达二十多年的考古发掘工作中，先后发现和出土的陶俑达七千余件，但是就其性别来讲，仅发现有男性，尚未见到女性和宦者俑。阳陵女性和宦者俑的出土不仅补全了秦汉陶俑的性别类型，由于阳陵出土的宦者俑是我国目前发现最早的同类实物资料，因而对中国古代宦官制度史的研究具有重要价值。

就陶俑的形态讲，现已发现有立俑、拱手立俑、执物立俑、跽坐俑、俯身俑、舞蹈俑、驭车俑、奏乐俑、行走俑、骑马俑等。就其身份可分为将军俑、步兵俑、骑兵俑、宦者俑、门吏俑、侍女俑、伎乐俑、驭手俑等。总之，可以认为阳陵陶俑品种丰富、门类齐全、数量极多，作为地下陵墓中的随葬品，这些陶俑应是除了皇家以外西汉社会各个阶层的代表，具有相当高的研究价值。

根据对出土的大量陶俑的分析研究可知，阳陵着衣式陶俑的制作工艺大致如下：一、模制：先选定合适的陶土，并经过筛选、淘洗使之更为纯净，然后将之和为干湿软硬适度的陶泥，再将其压嵌进事先准备好的模具内。当时的模具分为头颅、躯干、腿、脚四大段。二、加塑：陶俑的主体部分压模成型后再将诸如鼻、耳、阳具等小部件粘接上去，并将鼻、耳、肛门等人体窍孔插成很深的孔洞。为了避免模制出的陶俑千人一面的弊病，工匠们还对其面部进行了捏、塑、刻等艺术加工，使同模的陶俑形象各具情态。最后将俑体的各部分粘接成型。三、焙烧：待陶俑粗坯的制作完成后，将之放入陶窑内焙烧，使之变为坚硬的陶质。四、着色：将焙烧好的陶俑根据真人身体每一部分的实际情况为其绘彩，譬如陶俑的头发、眉毛、眼睛、胡须等绘为赭黑色，而其颜面、躯体则绘为橙红色。值得一提的是工匠们在绘彩时，对陶俑的面部又进行了划、抹、绘等进一步的艺术深加工，使之更加生动逼真。五、烘烤：为了使陶俑身上绘制的色彩附着更紧密，再将之二次入炉烘烤。六、雕琢：在制作陶质躯干的同时，制作带有关节并可以活动的木制臂膊和手。七、组装：将雕琢好的木制臂膊和手安装在事先烧制好的陶俑肩部预留的贯通两侧的圆孔处，至此一件陶俑的基本造型就算完成。接下来的工作是根据需要给陶俑穿着服装、配置装备等，例如阳陵南、北区从葬坑是按军阵设置的，其中需要大量的军士俑，于是作坊里那些已经完工的陶俑便被穿上战袍，披上铠甲，双手执戟拥盾，装扮成一幅威风凛凛的武士形象，然后按当时军队的建制放入从葬坑中。

与阳陵帝陵附近出土的着衣式陶俑相比，那些在建筑遗址、陪葬墓中出土的塑衣式陶俑制作工艺相对简单，大致经过了模制、加塑、焙烧、着色等阶段，减少了雕琢和组装等工序。塑衣式陶俑在进行其第一道工序模制时，陶俑身着的衣物等均与主体躯干一起压模成型。令西汉最高统治者刘启们所始料不及的是，经过两千多年历史的磨蚀，高级别、“衣纨绨”的着衣式陶俑木臂均残、彩衣尽蚀，显现出赤身裸体的“丑陋”形象；而级别较低的塑衣式陶俑则风采依旧，使我们不但能够领略到汉代陶塑人体美的韵味，同时也能观赏到文景盛世的灿烂衣冠。

阳陵陶俑中着衣式陶俑数量极大，这些赋彩着衣的陶俑经过在地下两千多年的埋藏后，肩上木制胳膊和身上的纺织品服装等大多已朽没无存，但是经过考古工作者精心的观察和清理，其服饰痕迹还是历历可辩。根据这些痕迹并参照塑衣式陶俑的服饰，我们就不难对阳陵陶俑的服饰情况有一个大致的了解。

1、发型：古人一般都留长发，只有囚犯才被剃去须发，名谓“髡首”。秦律中记载，斩人发髻和拔人须眉要判完旦（四年刑），斗殴时拔去别人的须发也要受到惩处，足以见得当时人们对须发的重视程度。阳陵陶俑头发均梳理得整整齐齐，发髻有椎髻、扁髻、圆髻等不同式样，真实的反应了汉代的生活习俗。

（1）椎髻：将全部头发向后梳理拢于脑后，在发稍处绾结。这种下垂式的发髻在秦汉时期的妇女发式中，一直占主导地位，因其形状与木椎相似而得名。阳陵的着衣式陶俑中的女俑皆梳此种发式，但个别男武士俑亦有梳椎髻者。《汉书·陆贾传》：“贾至，尉佗魋结箕踞见贾。”服虔注：“魋音椎，今兵士椎头髻也。”可见当时的兵士中确亦有梳椎髻者。

（2）堕马髻：又称堕髻。梳挽时由正中开缝，分发双颞，至颈后集为一股，挽髻之后垂至背部，另从髻中抽出一绺，朝一侧下垂。这种发式始于汉代，风行一时，东汉以后梳者渐少，至魏晋时几近绝迹，是妇女发式中较为讲究的一种。陪葬墓园130号墓出土的彩绘女俑所梳都是这种发髻。

（3）扁髻：阳陵出土的男武士俑、男侍从俑以及部分骑兵俑，都在脑后绾结扁髻。扁髻从形状上区分大致有两种：一是辫形扁髻，二是未编成辫形的扁髻。辫形扁髻的绾结方法有两种：一是把全部头发拢于脑后，编成一条宽辫，再将宽辫上折贴于脑后，上端与头顶平齐，有的略高出头顶，发稍处绾成一个小髻，髻内插笄；另一种绾结方法是：梳理时由中间开缝，将头发分成两部分，至两颞处分别编成六至七根小辫，再把辫子向上折起，至脑后集为一股，挽髻后插笄将辫子固定于脑后发层上。这种发式皆见于南区从葬坑出土的骑兵俑头上。未编成辫形的扁髻梳理相对较为简单，绾结方法是：把头发梳理后全部拢于脑后，然后将发上折反贴于脑后，再将高出头顶的余发盘结成髻。髻内横插笄固定。

（4）圆髻：阳陵南区从葬坑出土的骑马俑中，有一类颧骨似馒头状凸出者，其发髻也比较特殊。俑头上没有编织发辫，只是在脑后绾着圆丘形的发髻。绾结的方法是：将头发梳理整齐后全部拢于脑后弯成环形，将其余的头发绕环一周塞入环内，再将发尾压在绕环一周的发股之下。这种发髻古之名称不详。因其形似圆丘，故暂称之为圆髻。

2、冠式：南区从葬坑出土的许多陶俑头部，均残留着丝织品的痕迹。可以肯定其中一部分俑是戴冠的，但由于保存的缘故，多数俑的冠式已不详。这里仅从南区从葬坑20号坑出土的两件俑头上的丝织品痕迹对武士俑的冠式做一分析推测。这两件陶俑的头饰保存相对较好，俑头的额部经两鬓至枕骨部，有一圈宽约两厘米的朱红色印迹，十分鲜艳。从颜色上残留的经纬编织纹观察，似为丝织品残迹。此物大概就是束敛头发的“陌额”。《汉书·周勃传》记薄太后“以冒絮提文帝”。应劭注“陌额，絮也”。古人多蓄长发，在梳理之后用布帛扎额，称之“陌额”，作用与今天的发带大抵相似。俑头上戴冠，形状犹如倒扣的簸箕，圆顶，前沿（额部）较短，后沿（脑后）较深，两侧各有一条长耳。冠上孔眼分明，是用细疏的布帛制作而成的。这种冠类似古代的弁，《释名·释首饰》说：“弁，如两手合时也。”《续汉书·舆服志》则谓：弁“制如覆杯，前高广，后卑锐。”可见弁的形状犹如两手相扣，或者像一只反转的耳杯。以此来看，阳陵汉俑头上所戴就是弁。先秦以来，武士主要戴弁。《周礼·司服》说：“凡兵事，韦弁服。”陕西省咸阳杨家湾汉墓陪葬坑出土的大批带有陶塑服饰的兵马俑，也在头上戴弁，与阳陵着衣式陶俑的冠式十分接近。

3、衣裳：就社会风习而言，汉代人以袍服为重，多着长衣，这一点在阳陵出土的塑衣式陶俑上表现的十分清楚。这类陶俑身上所塑服装结构明晰，衣着穿法清楚，大致有以下几点特征：一、衣裳相连，在腰间合缝；二、矩领，即领式为方折式样；三、衣襟接长一段，作成斜角，着时由前绕至背后，以免露出里衣。这些都是长衣的基本特征。长衣又名“深衣”，出现于春秋之际，盛行于战国、西汉，无论男女、尊卑均可穿着，因其被体深邃而得名。阳陵塑衣式陶俑无论其性别、身份如何，均身着深衣，这就进一步说明了当时深衣制的盛行。

阳陵着衣式陶俑身上的衣服多已腐朽，式样难辩。单就南区从葬坑出土的着衣式陶俑而言，其身份应为武士，需要行军作战，而汉代的深衣、袍服一般不开衩口，且袖口肥大，行走不甚方便，因此让其着深衣或袍服就不太现实了。在秦始皇陵和杨家湾汉墓出土的塑衣武士俑中，多数陶俑均穿长度仅达膝部的长襦。长襦与袍服的主要区别是长度不同，深衣、袍服长度及足，而长襦的长度仅及膝部。从南区从葬坑清理中发现的裸俑衣物残迹来看，阳陵着衣武士俑的上衣也就是仅及膝部附近，穿的也应该是长襦。这种衣服比较短，袖口也较窄，便于行动和劳作，所以着衣武士俑身穿长襦是合乎当时实际的。

在大部分武士俑的小腿部位还缠有朱红色织物，并有斜绕痕迹，显然是系有“行縢”。汉军的行縢

是用大块布帛，四角缀带，先横束于带的上方，再斜绕而下呈“Z”形，扎结紧固于腿下。《释名》说“幅，所以自偪束，今谓行縢，言以裹腿。”这种行縢，就是近代军队中战士包扎的裹腿。杨家湾汉墓的骑兵和步兵俑群以及秦俑坑内武士俑的胫部亦扎着形制与此相仿的行縢，证明在秦汉时此种服制比较流行。

4、甲胄：南区从葬坑还出土了大量的披甲武士俑，由于甲片原为皮质，出土时已朽，仅存棕红色和黑色的痕迹。清理迹象表明，铠甲的甲片为正方形，边长2厘米，每边的中部有2个小孔用以连接上下左右的甲片。铠甲领部的甲片排列为上压下，左压右。铠甲的长度略短于长襦，由腰部分为上下两部分。前甲上部甲片由中线向外压，上压下共有六层，用绳子连接。前甲下部为上小下大的喇叭形，下压上共有四层，均为左压右。后甲中线两侧甲片的排列方法与前甲正相反。披膊部分只有两层甲片。(33)这类甲由于其甲片形似一枚简札，故文献中称之为札甲。汉代披甲武士俑的形象，以杨家湾汉墓陪葬坑所出陶俑反映的最为具体。这里的俑大多都披札甲，简单的类型仅护住胸、背，复杂一些的增加披膊和垂于腰下的腹甲。(34)杨家湾汉墓陪葬坑的时代和性质与阳陵南区从葬坑大体相当，结合清理时发现的迹象来看，阳陵的披甲武士俑的甲式也与其类同。

5、鞋履：秦汉时期的鞋履，主要有履、舄、屩、鞋、靴等，但在正规场合，汉代人应着履。阳陵塑衣式陶俑足上所穿，基本上应为履。着衣式陶俑足部虽然未发现有鞋履的痕迹，但从其它部位的着衣情况推断，应该不会忽略足部的穿着。与其性质近似的杨家湾汉墓陪葬坑所出陶俑脚上所穿鞋履，大致有四种：草履式的“芒鞋”，方口翘尖的“黻履”、浅帮圆口鞋和高腰绣花靴。(35)阳陵着衣式陶俑的鞋履式样也应与上述杨家湾陶俑基本相似，一般武士俑多着草履，骑兵俑着浅帮圆口鞋，其余两种可能较少。

从制作技术和造型风格来看，阳陵陶俑应是两种不同文化和埋葬制度影响的产物。阳陵大量随葬陶俑及塑衣式陶俑的工艺造型与秦始皇兵马俑坑出土的陶俑基本一致，无疑受到了秦帝陵殉葬制度的影响，而多数塑衣式陶俑身着的“深衣”则是楚文化的明显特征之一。

着衣式陶俑加装臂膀，外着丝帛衣服的作法，明显地与秦俑不同，这种制法目前所见的只有楚俑。在湖北江陵雨花台、湖南长沙等处楚墓中，多有这类着衣木俑出土。这种习俗后来被原楚国疆域内的西汉墓所沿袭。建国后发掘的湖南长沙马王堆曾出土有两件戴冠着衣男俑、十件着衣女仆俑和八件着衣歌舞俑，俑体均为木制，躯干仅刻出轮廓，均无双臂，身着罗绮所制的衣物。(36)这些西汉木俑明显是承袭了楚俑的造型风格。据此，可以确定阳陵出土的裸体着衣式陶俑，也应是楚风影响下的产物。

阳陵陶塑动物主要有马、牛、羊、狗、猪、鸡等，这些动物俑为畜类，但其制作工艺也相当讲究，它既经过了类似塑衣式陶俑模制、加塑、焙烧、着色等加工工序，亦采用了着衣式陶俑制作中的雕琢、组装等工艺（牛、羊、马等的犄角、尾巴为木制组装）。阳陵的陶塑动物种类繁多，栩栩如生，极富生活情趣。陶牛身壮体硕，四腿强健，颈部粗短，双耳斜伸，两眼外鼓，体现出一股倔强有力的牛气。陶绵羊躯体浑圆，双腿细长，两耳斜垂，口微张，臀肥大，尾下垂。陶山羊身躯圆润，腿直如柱，竖耳，胡须下垂，小尾上翘，神态安祥，呈现出一副温顺可爱之态。陶猪膘肥体胖，四肢矮壮，大腹下垂，腹下有两排乳头，脖

颈粗短，长嘴大耳，憨态可掬。陶犬分狼犬、家犬两种，狼犬两耳斜竖，双目虎视前方，嘴巴较细长，两腮外鼓，脖颈较短，身躯壮实，四肢有力，长尾下垂。家犬两耳直竖，双目略外鼓，嘴巴较粗短，身躯肥硕，四肢粗壮，尾巴上卷。二犬造型生动，刻划传神，给人以凛然不可侵犯之神态。陶鸡分雌雄两种。通体彩绘，色彩鲜艳。雄鸡昂首翘尾，长喙小眼，朱红色高冠，黑、红、黄三色羽毛。母鸡形体较小，尾巴较短，头部无高冠，神形俱佳、惟妙惟肖。阳陵陶塑动物数量之大、造型之美，是前所未见的。(37)

由各类陶俑和动物雕塑组成的阳陵陶塑不仅是西汉社会包括政治、经济、军事、文化等在内的全方位的信息载体，对我们了解、掌握、研究汉代历史具有重要的史料价值；同时也有着较高的艺术价值。就目前尚未全面展开的初步研究来看，阳陵陶塑一方面继承了秦俑"写实的艺术风格"、"人体的造型特征"、"神韵的重视"、"娴熟的技法"、"绘塑结合的技法"和"制作工艺的多样化" 等艺术传统，(38)同时又在其基础上摈弃了前代呆板生硬的模式，汲取了楚文化的造型艺术精华，创造出"写意的艺术表现手法"、"绘、塑、雕、着结合的技法"、"形体的重视" 和 "浪漫主义的手法" 等艺术特征，转向生动精细，富有生活情趣的时代新风，使我国古代雕塑艺术发展到一个新的阶段。

(1)《汉书 · 食货志》

(2)《汉书 · 景帝纪》

(3)《汉书 · 景帝纪》

(4)《汉书 · 外戚传》

(5)焦南峰：《汉代京城、帝陵的考古发掘和研究》、待刊稿。

(6)秦中行：《汉阳陵附近钳徒墓的发现》，《考古》，1976年12期。

(7)王丕忠、张子波、孙德润：《汉景帝阳陵调查简报》，《考古与文物》，1980年第一期。

(8)刘庆柱、李毓芳：《西汉诸陵调查与研究》，《文物资料丛刊》，第六辑，1982年。刘庆柱、李毓芳：《西汉十一陵》，陕西人民出版社1987年7月。

(9)陕西省考古研究所汉陵考古队：《汉景帝阳陵南区从葬坑第一号简报》，《文物》，1992年第四期。陕西省考古研究所汉陵考古队：《汉景帝阳陵南区从葬坑第二号简报》，《文物》，1994年第四期。陕西省考古研究所汉陵考古队：《中国汉阳陵彩俑》陕西旅游出版社，1992年。

(10)焦南峰、王保平、马永嬴、李岗等：《汉景帝阳陵发现陪葬墓园》，《中国文物报》，1999年11月14日。《汉阳陵园内发现大批从葬坑出土大量珍贵文物》，《中国文物报》，1999年11月28日。

(11)陕西省考古研究所阳陵考古队：《汉景帝阳陵考古新发现》，《文博》，1999年第6期。

(12)焦南峰、王保平、马永嬴、李岗：《汉阳陵园内发现大批从葬坑出土大量珍贵文物》，《中国文物报》，1999年11月28日。

(13)发掘尚未结束，资料存阳陵考古队。

(14)同上

(15)同上

(16)焦南峰、王保平、马永嬴、李岗：《汉阳陵园内发现大批从葬坑出土大量珍贵文物》，《中国文物报》，1999年11月28日。

(17)陕西省考古研究所阳陵考古队：《汉景帝阳陵考古新发现》，《文博》，1999年第六期。

(18)陕西省考古研究所汉陵考古队：《中国汉阳陵彩俑》陕西旅游出版社，1992年。

(19)董鸿闻等《阳陵罗经石的实测和研究》，《测绘通报》，1995年6期。

(20)焦南峰：《汉代京城、帝陵的考古发掘和研究》、待刊稿。

(21)秦中行：《汉阳陵附近钳徒墓的发现》，《考古》，1976年12期。

(22)《汉书 · 高惠高后文功臣表》。

(23)焦南峰、王保平、马永嬴、李岗：《汉景帝阳陵发现陪葬墓园》，《中国文物报》，1999年11月14日。

(24)焦南峰、马永嬴：《西汉帝陵无昭穆制度论》，《文博》，1999年5期。

(25)赵化成：《从"商周公墓制"到秦汉"独立陵园制"的历史轨迹》，《古代文明研究通讯（摘要）》，2000年六期。

(26)焦南峰：《汉代京城、帝陵的考古发掘和研究》，待刊稿。

(27)孙机：《汉代物质文化资料图说 · 阙，阙门》，《文物出版社》，1991年。

(28)重庆市文化局、重庆市博物馆：《四川汉代石阙》，文物出版社，1992年。

(29)焦南峰：《汉家陵阙》，《中国文物报》，1999年11月30日。

(30)李岗：《汉阳陵围棋棋局》，《中国文物报》，1999年12月5日。

(31)王学理：《着衣式木臂陶俑的时代意义》，《文博》，1997年第六期。

(32)资料存阳陵考古队。

(33)陕西省考古研究所汉陵考古队：《汉景帝阳陵南区从葬坑第二号简报》，《文物》，1994年第四期。

(34)杨秉礼、史宇阔等：《西汉三千彩绘兵马俑》，陕西人民美术出版社，1996年。

(35)杨秉礼、史宇阔等：《西汉三千彩绘兵马俑》，陕西人民美术出版社，1996年。

(36)湖南省博物馆、中国社会科学院考古研究所《长沙马王堆一号汉墓》，文物出版社，1973年。

(37)王保平：《精美的汉代动物雕塑》，《中国文物报》，1999年11月30日。

(38)袁仲一：《秦始皇陵兵马俑研究》，文物出版社，1990年。

The Yangling Mausoleum of Emperor Jingdi of the Western Han Dynasty

Since 1990's, the Shaanxi Archaeological Research Institute has undertaken extensive archaeological survey, drilling and excavations, yielding in remarkable achievements in this endeavour. The Yangling Archaeological Exhibition Center was open to public on October 1, 1999. In order to provide experts in this area with an overview of our findings so as to deepen the archaeological research of the Han mausoleum, and to familiarize our visitors with the glory and grandeur of "the Great Reign of Emperors Wendi and Jingdi", we have edited this brochure for the keen readers.

1. An Overview of the History and Geography of Yangling

Emperor Jingdi (the Prospect Emperor), the fourth emperor of the Western Han Dynasty, is named Liu Qi. He was born in the 7th reigning year of Emperor Huidi (188 B.C.) and was enthroned at the age of 32. During the 17 years of his reign, he did his best to follow the historical trend and ruled wisely. While continuing to follow the policies and philosophical ideas of the Yellow Emperor and Laozi (also spelt "Laozu") and the Daoist (also spelt "Taoist") philosophy of "*wuwei*", (literally meaning "doing nothing", but what it really means is to follow the natural course), he adopted the policy of "giving the people time to recuperate". The revolt by the seven kingdoms was crushed during his reign. Externally, he adopted the policy of "pacifying the Huns through marriages". These wise policies safeguarded the nation's peace and security, strengthened the rule of the central government and promoted the development of the economy so that after the initial prosperity of the reign of Emperor Han Wendi, the realm saw the first zenith in the history of the development of feudal China characterized by wise policies, peace in the land, a thriving economy and contentment and increased livelihood of the people.

Yangling is the mausoleum where Emperor Jingdi and his empress were buried in the same mausoleum but in separate tombs. In 153 B.C. during the reign of Emperor Jingdi, "the name of the county of Yiyang was changed into Yangling"[1] which was designated for their mausoleum. "The Emperor died at Weiyang palace in 142 B.C., and was buried in February the next year."[2] "Empress Xiaojing, surnamed Wang, was the mother of Emperor Wudi, the Martial Emperor. Fifteen years after the death of her husband (126 B.C.), she died and was buried at Yangling by the side of her husband's tomb."[3]

Yangling is located in the Xian'yang Heights to the north of the villages of Zhangjiawan and Hougoucun in the town of Zhengyang, Xian'yang City, Shaanxi Province. Lying on the border area of Weicheng district, Jingyang and Gaoling counties, it reaches the Jing River in the north and extends across the Wei River to border on Chang'an County; on its eastern side, the two rivers the Jing and the Wei converge, and on its west it borders on Changling, the mausoleum of Emperor Gaozu, or the High Progenitor.

2. The History of Archaeological Excavations at Yangling

Scientific survey of Yangling in the sense of modern archaeology really began in the 1970's. In 1972 experts from Shaanxi Historical Museum discovered and located the site of the graveyard of the convict labourers at Yangling after conducting trial drilling there.[4] And then in 1978, archaeologists from Xian'yang Municipal Museum underwent archaeological survey at Yangling including the tombs of the emperor and empress, the original sites of the gates of the enclosures and some accompanying burial pits.[5] In 1980's again, experts from the Chinese Academy of Sciences went on a more extensive survey of the mausoleum area with remarkable achievements.[6]

Between May 1990 and October 1994, in cooperation with the building of the special express way for Xian'yang Airport, the Han Yangling Archaeological team of the Shaanxi Provincial Archaeological Research Institute began to undertake, on a larger scale, archaeological research and drilling. In the course of five years, they uncovered two accompanying burial pits and the ruins of some architectural structures. This done, they proceeded to conduct excavation at part of the burial pit in the southern area of the mausoleum.[7] The excavation shows that the burial pit has a unique layout with a rich wealth of well preserved relics particularly those of pottery figurines. These finds are listed as one of China's ten major archaeological discoveries in 1990.

Since 1995, based on the past achievements, the Yangling archaeological team undertook on an ambitious scale surveying, mapping, drilling and excavations, which further revealed the layout and scale and the pattern of the emperor's tomb, and a multitude of accompanying graveyards. The excavations also uncovered the ruins of the south gate of the original wall that enclosed the mausoleum, a number of medium sized and small sized accompanying burial pits and, in the course of the archaeological diggings, more than 9,300 relics were unearthed yielding up rich fruit in this endeavour.[8]

On October 1, 1999, the Yangling Archaeological Exhibition Center, following its completion, was open to public, thus ushering in a new page of archaeological excavation, research, protection and its development as a tourism spot of the mausoleum of Yangling.

3. Major Events of the Archaeological Excavations at Yangling.

Excavations have revealed that the mausoleum of Yangling is roughly shaped like a goud: it's about 6 km from east to west and between 1 and 3 km from noth to south, covering an area of 12 square km. The mausoleum is comprised of the tombs of the emperor and empress, the accompanying burial pits in the north and south areas, the graveyard of the convict labourers, temples and other archetectural structures of rites, accompanying graveyards and the town of Yangling. The emperor's tomb faces east; it is situated in the middle of the mausoleum slighly to the western side. The empress's tomb, the accompanying burial pits of the south and north areas and the foundation of the No. One architectural structure are arrayed with equal distances at the four corners of the emperors's tomb. The accompanying tombs of the comcubines and the pelorus, which stand in parallel with each other, are located to the south and north of the emperor's tomb respectively.The graves of the convict labourers and the sites of three architectural structures lie to the west of the emperor's tomb, and they are arranged in a column from north to south. The accompanying graveyards, arranged like the squares of a chessboard, lie on both sides of *simadao*, the mausoleum's main path, on the eastern side of the emperor's tomb. The entire mausoleum is neatly arranged and it centers round the emperor's tomb surrounded by four corners; the clusters of structures and burial pits are connected from east to west and are in parallel with one another from north to south. All these show the absolute authority of the monarque and the rigidly stratified feudal society of ancient China. The plane figure of the mausoleum is shaped like a square with each side measuring 417.5-418 meters. There are walls of tamped earth between 3-3.5m in width surrounding the mausoleum. Each of these walls has three gates adjacent to one another; but there are no rostrums at the four corners of these walls. In the middle of the mausoleum is the sealed entrance which is shaped like a flat topped piramid which measures 167. 5-168.5 m. long each side at its base; the space of the base is bigger than that of the top. The mausoleum faces east and is shaped like the Chinese character 亞.

Initial drilling on both sides of the four passages which lie outside the sealed entrance revealed 86 accompanying burial pits of which 21 are on the eastern flank, 21 on the northern flank, 20 on the western and 19 on the southern. The burial pits on the eastern and western flanks are arrayed from east to west, and those on the nothern and southern flanks are arrayed from north to south. There is also five burial pits on the northeastern corner arranged in a column from north to south. The pits average 3-4m in width. The longest pit measures over 100m while the shortest measures only 4m. All the pits are about 3m in depth and the bottom of these pits are about 8-14m from the present day ground level. The drilling has also shown a multitude of pottery figurines of cavalrymen, foot soldiers, animals, living utensils made of earthenwear or bronz or lackwear, and weaponry, carriages and various kinds of equipment for horses and chariots.[9]

Between 1998 and 1999, we conducted exploratory drilling at part of the burial pits No. 11, No. 13 and No. 19. The No. 13 pit is shaped like a rectangular box; it is 92 meters long, 3 meters wide and 3 meters in depth. Shaped like a tunnel with a wooden framework, it measures approximately 8 meters from the bottom of the pit to the ground level. The structure was built as in accordance to the following procedures: first the ground was leveled, then earth was piled on top of it till it was some 0.6 to 0.7 meters high. Then the piled earth was tamped as layers of earth was heaped on it. This done, the piled earth was dug in through several layers of subsoil until it reached the deep earth some 7 meters from the ground. After the bottom of the pit was roughly leveled, two flat sided timbers were laid on the two sides of the earthen pit ,the top of which was covered with planks which served as the floor. On the wooden floor was erected wooden pillars which in turn supported the beams on the two sides of the ceiling. Planks were then laid on the beams which in turn were covered with matresses. The planks on the ceiling were on the same level with the ground. In this way a huge hollow like an underground tunnel was made in which burial objects were laid. The last procedure was to seal the entrance with square wooden columns. On top of the burial pit is a layer of tamped earth about 3.5-6 meters in width. Above it is a layer of modern accumulation which is covered with subsoil of farmland. The No. 11 and

No. 19 pits are 74m and 20m long respectively, and the width, depth and structure and strata of these two pits resemble or coincide with those of the No. 13 pit.

The area in the No. 13 pit that has been excavated on a trial basis measures 22 meters in length. After the top ceiling was cleared out, a multitude of densely arrayed pottery animal figurines facing the emperor's mausoleum was revealed. The area can be divided into four sections according to the kinds of animals. Section one, positioned at the eastern end of the pit, is 7 meters long, and in it were uncovered 235 pottery goats coloured in black and orange. To the west of the first section is section two measuring 7 meters too, and in it were found 458 coloured pottery dogs which fall into two kinds: wolfhounds and dogs. These are coloured in yellow, white, black, grey and orange. It's interesting to note that the lips and noses of some of the dogs are painted red. Beside section two and further to the west are section three and four, both measuring near 8 meters. In section three in the northern half were unearthed 33 coloured sheep in six columns painted in black and pink. In the southern half were unearthed 54 pottery piglets arrayed in two columns coloured in black and white. The piglets with long noses and pricked up ears and tiny tails look lively and vivid and are very true to life. These animals are partitioned by wooden planks underneath them, and still underneath the planks are more coloured pottery figurines.[10]

An area of 24 square meters in Pit No. 11 was excavated, on an exploratory basis too, in which were found four columns of pottery cavalrymen. They face the east gate of the mausoleum with their backs towards the emperor's tomb. Between each two columns of cavalrymen are wooden carriages. The burial objects unearthed include 26 pottery cavalrymen, 17 painted wooden horses ,4 wooden carriages and bronze and iron weapons and equipment of the horses and carriages numbering some hundred pieces in all.[11]

Of the No. 19 pit only 12 square meters have been excavated. From it were unearthed 4 wooden horses, 1 wooden carriage, some 20 odd pottery warriors, 10 pottery animal figurines and bronze and iron weapons and equipment used on the horses and carriages and pottery utensils totaling some 30 pieces. These objects are arranged in the following order: the wooden horses are placed in the fore front followed by the wooden carriages; the warriors are lined on both sides of the horses and carriages. At the back are placed the pottery animals and utensils lined on the two sides, too.[12]

In addition, in the hole cut by former tomb robbers in the No. 16 and No. 18 pits were found a seal bearing the inscriptions which read "*tai guan zhi yin*" (the seal of the food and drinks official) and figurines of eunuchs, which throw a light to the nature of the burial pit.[13]

The ruins of the south gate of Yangling is on the duesouth of the mausoleum 120 meters from the sealed entrance of the emperor's tomb. Excavation of the site was conducted between March and June of 1997, during which time 56 square earthen blocks sized 10m by 10m were excavated. The total area cleared covers 3,100 square meters, in which are found the remains of two architectural structures and 583 relics including flat shaped and round shaped tiles and cilinder shaped tiles with hollows in them, vertebrates, a chess board of *weiqi*—a chess game commonly known in the west as "go", a plate for gambling games, the head of a pounding device, etc.

The south gate is composed of two linked structures each with three lesser gates. The three lesser gates are all shaped in a rectangular progressively diminished in size. In the middle of the south gate is the main gate, around which are the four roofed structures—one on the eastern flank, one on the western, and the other two on the interior and exterior respectively. On the exterior structure is the main rostrum flanked by the lesser rostrum. The two rostrums were built with tamped earth covered with a mixture of straw and mud about 1-2cm in width; this mixture was then whitewashed with lime and, as the last procedure, painted with red. Round the platforms and rostrum were winding corridores, the floor of which were paved with square bricks. Outside the corridores were a layer of pebbles for preventing the earth outside the corridores from being washed away by rain. The pebbles outside the corridores tilted to the two sides so that the corridor assumes the shape of the vertebrate of a fish tilting down from the backbone. The whole structure was neatly designed with the two sides of the corridor parallel to each other. Grand in scale and well preserved, it is an invaluable architectural marvel of the Han period.[14]

The colours of the tamped earth that forms the basis of the platforms and the two rostrums of the south gate are distinctly different: the earth of the platforms is coloured in light brown while that of the rostrums in orange pink; obviously, they were not built at one time. The area at the joint of the tamped earth that made up the foundation and close to the side of the two rostrums is covered with a mixture of straw and mud and is whitewashed and pained in red—an evidence that the rostrums were built a bit earlier while the platforms were added later on. We should not be in great error to assume that the rostrums of the south gate were built at the same period of the mausoleum, that is to say, during the reign of Han Jingdi. As *The History of the Han (or Hanshu)* records that in lunar January of the third reigning year of Han Wudi (114 B. C.) a fire broke out at the Yangling Mausoleum. It is thus reasonable to assume that the building of the platforms occured after the great fire and during the reign of Wudi. This assumption is in accordance with the coins, and the flat, round and cylinder shaped tiles and other building materials unearthed over the years.

The ground area of the empress's tomb also assumes the shape of a square with each side measuring 347.5—350 meters. There are also walls of tamped earth on four sides with doors in each side. However, no rostrums have been found on the four corners of the walls. The sealed entrance is located in the middle of the mausoleum, which is shaped like a flat topped pyramid. Each side on the base of the mound measures 160 meters; the height measures 26.49 meters. The empress's tomb, facing east, also assumes the shape of the Chinese character 亞. In each of the four directions there is a tomb passage, the one on the eastern side being the widest and longest. There are also accompanying burial pits round the empress's tomb.[15]

The accompanying pits in the southern area lie to the southeast of the emperor's tomb or to the due south of the empress's tomb. The pits which occupy an area of 9,600 square meters have 14 columns and 24 subtracks arrayed from east to west. The plane figure of the pits assumes a horizontal line or the Chinese character 亞, both lying from north to south. They measure between 25m and 291m in length, 4m in width in the mojority of cases, and 20 meters between the columns. Between 1990 and 1997, exploratory excavations or, in some cases, complete excavation were conducted in 14 burial pits, in which were found neatly arrayed pottery worriors, granaries, pottery figurines of cows, goats, pogs, dogs and chickens, and living utensils made of earthnwear, iron and bronz, which serve as an epitome of the military life of the Han period; they may also suggest the North and South Armies respectively.[16]

The pelorus ruins are situated to the southeast of the emperor's tomb where the terrain is elevated but progressively tilts down to all sides. Archaeological excavation reveals that the area roughly assumes the shape of a square about 260 meters long each side. There is a ditch round the ruins. At the highest point of the area is placed a huge square rock which the local people call *luojingshi*—the pelorus. Cut out of a monolithic block of black mica, the pelorus measures 183cm north and south and 180cm east and west, and its width is 40cm. On top of the stone is a disk on high relief. In the disk is carved a cross-shaped slot which measures approximately 2.3 cm both in length and depth. As has been determined after surveying, the cross points to due north and due south respectively.[17] It can be inferred with reasonable safety that the pelorus was used for determining the level ground, height and position in the course of the construction of the mausoleum. And it is the earliest known stone for surveying and mapping in the world. While conducting exploratory excavation we found in the middle of the ruins was a raised platform of tamped earth. It is reasonable to infer that it was the foundation of a main building which measures 54 meters in circumference. There were 12 doors, three in each side. Around the platform were found a brick-paved floor and pebbles for preventing the earth underneath the eaves from being washed away by raindrops, hollowed tiles carved with four mythical animals, piles of broken tiles and other remains. The architectural ruins in this place are located on the elevated ground and they are neatly arranged and grand in scale. We will not be in great error to assume that this was one of the important architectural structures for rites of the Yangling mausoleum.[18]

Discovered in the early 1970's, the graveyard of the convict labourers lies about 1.5 km to the northeast of the emperor's tomb, extending an area of 80,000 square meters. It is estimated that as many as over 10,000 convict labourers were buried there. Twenty-nine such graves were excavated in 1972 in which were found 35 human skeleton remains. These graves were not orderly arranged, and the skeletons, piling one one another, were in a terrible mess. No burial objects were found there. Most of these skeletons were found with chains and shackles, some even exhibiting obvious traces of cuts from knives and axes.[19]

Clusters of architectural structures were also found within the compounds of the emperor's and empress's tombs, in the north and west of the emperor's tomb, and in the south of the accompanying burial pits. Hopefully, future excavations will yield more details of the mysteries lying underground.

The accompanying burial graveyard which lies 1,100 meters to the east of the emperor's tomb on the western end and its eastern end extends to the elevated land of Mijiaxia village. It stretches 2,350 meters covering an area of 3.5 square meters. There is a ditch running from north to south on the eastern and western sides of the pit respectively which served as the boundaries of the pit. Across the pit and in the middle is the main path of the mausoleum with numerous accompanying graves lying on both sides of the pit. To date, as many as 107 accompanying graveyards have been found which are arrayed in 16 columns and separated by the ditches. More than 5,000 graves have been found in these yards of which 337 graves have been cleared up. A total of 5516 cultural relics have been unearthed of which are 1283 pottery pieces including round or square shaped containers, pots, granaries, stoves, tripods and earthen bowl; 772 bronze objects including coins marked with banliang, *wuzhu*, big *qian* 50, and lesser *qian* (all these are units of the face value of the coins), mirrors, buckles, equipment for horses and carriages, shooting devices called *nu*, seals and tiny ornaments, 2932 bronze coins, 212 iron objects including swords, axes, lamps, curved knives; 54 jade objects including *yugui* (for recording events), *yuhan* (to be placed underneath the tongue of the dead body), jade cicadas, jade lids etc., and 102 objects made of other materials ranging from bone, shell, to stone and lacquer.

According to the layout and burial style of the graveyard and as is in accordance to the analyses of the above unearthed relics, these graveyards can be divided into three periods—the early, the middle and the later periods.

Thirty of them may as well be called graveyards of the early period, which are arrayed in two columns on both sides of the mausoleum's main path and which are mostly shaped in rectangular in their plane figures with the two short sides facing east and west, some roughly assuming the shape of a square. Averagely there are one to five graves in each of these graveyards. The main grave assumes the shape of the Chinese character 甲 by which side are usually found accompanying pits. The passages in the main graves of the graveyards to the south of the main passage, or *simadao*, all point to the north while those of the graveyards to the north of simadao, point to the south. In these graveyards a total of 60 graves of the Han period have been excavated in which 1652 relics have been unearthed. In one grave(97YPIY$_9$-GYM$_{130}$) in particular, which lies in the first column south of simadao, the mausoleum's main passage, a copper seal bearing the inscriptions of "Zhou Ying" has been unearthed. It has been verified after we referred to *The Book of the Han*, that there were two Zhou Yings during the reign of Han Jingdi. One was the Duke of Zhou Die's son whom Han Jingdi made the Duke of Dan and, after the latter's death, was conferred with the honorary title of the Duke of Kang. The other was the grandson of Zhou Cheng, Duke of Gaojing. The grandson was, after the death of Zhou Cheng, created the Duke of Sheng, which had been the feufdom of the grandfather's. Thus it is safe to infer that the owner of the grave 97YPIY$_9$-GYM$_{130}$ is either Zhou Ying, the Duke of Dan or Zhou Ying, the Duke of Sheng.[20] In another grave (97YPIY$_9$-GYM$_{144}$) which also lies in the first column south of the simadao, were unearthed a number of bronze objects including a round container, a square container, and a basin. On the side of the round bronze container, are inscribed 17 characters in four lines which read "The bronze container of *banyijia*, which means Banyi's house (or the noble house of the city of Ban), which has a dry volume of 10 *dou* and which weighs 35 *jin*. Made in the second workshop." "Banyi's house" which is akin to "Yangxin's house" was most probably the title of a duke or princess. Regrettabaly, historical records about "Banyi's house" have been hopelessly lost. Our inferences about the grave M130 and about Banyi's house, and the historical records about Priministers Li Cai and Su Jiang being buried in the accompanying graveyards in the mausoleum, all point to the assumption that the owners of the graves in the yard of that historical period are either princesses and other relatives of the emperor or the dukes, high ranking officials and other members of the aristocracy. We would, therefore, not be in great error to assume that the graveyard in this area is in fact the accompanying burial ground of the Yangling mausoleum, which is characterized by its proximity to the mausoleum's main passage, *simadao*, the neat planning, the wide and deep ditches, the huge size of the graves in it, the orderly arrangement and the high position of the owners.

There are 55 graveyards of the middle period. Neatly arrayed, they are located to the north and south of the graveyards of the earleir period and are separated from the latter by 10 meters. The plain figures of most graveyards in this area assume a square with the passages pointing to the north. In one of these yards were found remains of architectural structurs or pottery kilns. The eastern and western sides of the graveyards, which are in straight lines, were obviously planned and constructed at one time. Most of the ditches that lie from north to south are in one straight line. The graves in these yards are mostly median or small sized; in some of the yards there are more graves while in others less. In the graveyard of this area, a total of 120 graves have been excavated in which 1850 cultural relics have been found. A special feature underlying the middle period graveyards is that while neatly arranged, they lie farther away from the mausoleum's main passage, *simadao*; the ditches around these are narrow and shallow; that while there is a multitude of burial objects the graves are noticeably small as compared with those of the earlier period and that the owners of the graves were of less prominent social position.

As in accordance to historical records, the positions of the graves and to the analysis of the unearthed relics, the accompanying graves of the Han Yangling were built during the reign of Han Jingdi, too, that is, during the early period of the Han. (The building of the graves extended to the middle period of the Eastern Han, as is the case with some of the accompanying graves.) It is safe, thus, to infer that the graves there in the early period are between the time when Jingdi began to construct his mausoleum and the time during the reign of Wudi; that those of the middle period belong to the middle and later part of the Western Han; and that those of the later period belong to the later years of the Western Han, extending all the way to the middle of the Eastern Han.[21]

4. The archaeological significance of excavating the Yangling Mausoleum

The first and foremost achievement is that the excavations have provided us with a familiarity of the overall layout of the mausoleum. Over the past thirty years, archaeologists have conducted numerous investigations, surveying and projecting, and have even undergone some exploratory excavations of the ground, the emperors' tombs, the accompanying graves, the burial pits and structurs in the eleven Western Han mausoleums with fruitful results. Particularly significant is that the mysteries of the burial system of the Western Dynasty have been unveiled thanks to the unremitting efforts of these experts. And this in turn will throw lights to the burial system of the other ten Western Han tombs.

For the first time in archaeological history the archaeologists have discovered that both the emperor's and empress's tombs of Yangling assume the Chinese character 亞 and that the tombs both face east. This discovery has solved the long controversy as to whether the Han tombs face south or east; the former assumption has now been dismissed that the Han tombs follow the system of King Zhou Mu. The findings, therefore, have solved a knotty problem in the research of the pattern of the mausoleums of the Han period.[22]

The Yangling finds involved in the drilling and exploratory excavations have raised new questions in these endeavors and have opened a new perspective for the research in the systems of the tombs of feudal emperors. The way these accompanying graves are positioned and arranged, and the burial objects are placed undoubtedly have a bearing on the style of the life of the royal family and the system of the imperil court. Therefore, the excavations we have conducted along with the ensuing research efforts have, to a great extent, contributed to the research into the above mentioned aspects of the court system.

The numerous accompanying graves neatly arrayed and with complete and elaborate ditches point to the fact that they had been carefully projected and planned. This in turn suggests that the layout and system of the accompanying graves of all the eleven Western Han tombs are similar to those in the Yangling mausoleum.

Basing on the data involved in the archaeological excavations and with reference to the findings of other emperors' tombs of the Western Han Dynasty, we can assume with reasonable safety that unlike the tombs and graves in the Shang and Zhou periods which were clustered together in a common cemetery, the Han tombs have enherited and further developed the layout and structure of the tomb of Emperor Qinshihuangdi—the First Emperor of All China, which has "an independant and multi functional mausoleum, grand in scale and intricated in structure". A new system of mausoleums was thus taking form which is in keeping with the social system of the Western Han Dynasty which "set a model for the mausoleum system of the emperors and kings of the autocratic feudal society of China for the next two thousand years".[23]

As a preliminary attempt, based on the findings and earlier analyses, the characteristics of the tombs of the Western Han period can now be summed up as follows:

1.Except for Baling which, by availing itself of the natural terrain, was built in the mountain cliff, the sealed entrances of other Western Han tombs were all made of tamped earth which are a square at the base and are shaped like a flat-topped pyramid; Only one tomb has two tiers with no architectural structure for offering sacrifice at the top.

2. All the emperors' tombs are shaped like the Chinese character 亞 facing east; among the four tomb passages which point to the east, west, north and south, only the east passages is the main one.

3. The emperor and the empress were buried in the same mausoleum but in separate tombs; the emperor's tomb which is bigger is located in the center while the empress's which is slightly smaller lies to the northeast of the emperor.

4. The tombs of the emperors and empresses of the early period of the Western Han are, in each case, located in the same mausoleum which covers a large area and is shaped in a rectangle. In the period after the building of Yangling the emperor' and empress's tombs are positioned in separated tomb areas with 450m-700m in between; they both assume a square in the base with each side measuring 400m for the emperor's mausoleum and 350m for the empress's respectively. Enclosing the mausoleums are walls made of tamped earth; in the middle of each wall is a gate. In the case of of the Yangling mausoleum, each of the four gates is comprised of three openings while each of the four gates at Duling consists of only two openings.

5. As a rule, between the sealed

entrances of the emperor's and empress's tombs and the walls lie a multitude of accompanying burial pits; some lie outside these mausoleums.

6. There are, without exception, temples and other architectural structures of rites in the mausoleums. The halls and bedrooms are usually positioned near or inside the mausoleums.

7. In the early and middle periods of the Western Han, towns are built in the vicinity of the emperor's mausoleums; and these towns are usually situated to the east or north of the mausoleums. The only exception was Emperor Hanyuandi who stopped the practice of building such towns.

8.Although accompanying burial graves appeared in earlier history it is those in the Western Han that are the grandest in scale. The accompanying burial graves in the Western Han mausoleums usually consist of two areas: most of those lie on the north or south side of *Simadao*- the main passage of the mausoleum and they are lined neatly from east to west or in columns from north to south; there are ditches separating these accompanying graves. The accompanying tombs of few exceptional concubines or other important figures are positioned on the north and south flanks of the emperor's mausoleums. The outer appearances of the accompanying tombs either assume a flat-topped pyramid or a bun, or a mini-mountain, depending on the rank and position of the owners and some other factors, too. Most of these tombs assume the shape of a bun while those taking the shape of a flat-topped pyramid come second in number; only few assume the shape of a mountain. Some of the accompanying tombs are surrounded by ditches. The plane figure of most of these accompanying graveyards assumes a square while a few assume a rectangle. In these graveyards are also found architectural remains such as villages, and halls for offering sacrifices. Around certain large scale accompanying tombs there are also a number of lesser graves and accompanying burial pits.

9. It can be inferred with reasonable safety that there are numerous convict graves around most of the Han mausoleums. The convict graveyard at Yangling which is separated from the other areas by a ditch lies some 1500m northwest of the emperor's tomb.[24]

The second greatest achievement in the course of the archaeological excavations of Yangling is the discovery of the south gate which has three openings. These openings in the gate are an important pattern in ancient architecture and they are often found in elaborate architectural pieces such as those outside the gates of the capital city wall, the imperial palaces and mausoleums. As recorded in the "Biography of Huo Guang",in *The Book of the Han* , "Huo Guang's widow expanded her late husband's tomb which had been built in his own time by erecting a gate of three openings." Thus we can see the gate with multiple openings continued as a pattern from the Western Han period. That means "an ordinary official could have in his tomb gate only a pair of single openings while dukes and higher ranking officials a pair of two openings—one being the main opening, and the other, the subordinate one". "The emperor could have a gate with three openings—the main opening plus two subordinate ones".[25]

Some experts are of the opinion that the gates with multiple openings occured way back in the Xia and Shang periods; however, there aren't any hard data or relics to substantiate this theory.[26] According to *Shijin*—The Classic of Poems and Zuozhuan, as an architectural form, gates with multiple openings appeared as early as the Western Zhou period. But again we lack unearthed relics to verify it. while there is a perplexing host of documents in the Spring and Autumn periods which record the existence of gates with three openings, archaeologists had so far found them only in pictures of stones and bricks belonging to the Eastern Han period and on the murals of the Dunhuang Grotto and the Tang tombs. With regards to actual relics, they have found stone gates with three openings of the Eastern Han period, and those at the Nipple Shaped Mountain of Qianling and at some Song tombs. But it is without a shadow of a doubt that it is the south gate at the mausoleum at Yangling that is the earliest in time, highest in rank and grandest in scale. Therefore, the excavation of the south gate of Yangling has greatly contributed to the research efforts in terms of the origin, evolution and significance in China's architectural history of the gates with multiple openings.[27] Also found at the south gate at Yangling are a pottery *weiqi* (an oriental chess game better known in the West as "go") chessboard, the ealiest of its kind, pottery vertebrate animals and the biggest flat tile (the remnant measures 108 by 43.5 mm.)[28]

Another great achievement of the archaeological excavations of Yangling is that a huge amount of pottery sculptures of various kinds have been unearthed. To date, a total number of 50,000 relics have been uncovered ranging from objects made of bronze, iron, gold, jade, stone, pottery, lacquer, wood, bone, shell, silk and hemp, to sample cereals such as wheat, millets, beans, yams, etc. Of all these unearthed relics, pottery objects including human and animal figurines are the greatest in number and most varied in kind.

The pottery figurines at Yangling fall to two types, i.e, those that originally were clothed[29] but presently nude figurines and those with clothes in high relief as part of the sculpture itself.

Nude figurines were found in the accompanying burial pit of the emperor's tomb, in the accompanying burial pits in the south area and in the burial pits of few large scale accompanying tombs; and those with clothes in bold relief are mostly found in the No. One architectural ruins and in the large or median scale accompanying tombs. We have found in recent years ruins of some pottery making kilns near Anling Mausoleum of Han Huidi, Maoling Mausoleum of Wudi and Duling Mausoleum of Xuandi, and the ancient city walls of the Han period. These archaeological findings have confirmed our hypotheses that the naked pottery figurines with wooden limbs were in coloured clothes at the time of burial and they were specially made as the superior type of burial objects for the royal family only; that ministers and ordinary members of the ariscratic families were not allowed to have these figurines for their use unless specially provided by the emperor himself—for them only pottery figures with clothes sculptured in bold relief could be used as burial objects.

Apart from male and female pottery figurines, we have also found figurines of eunuches[30] at Yangling—the first of its kind in the archaeological findings of the Qin and Han periods. The discovery of the eunuches has added sex content to the figurines hitherto unearthed and has contributed to an important extent to the research of the eunuch system in ancient China.

With regard to the postures of the figurines we have found standing figurines, and standing figurines with one hand cupping in another before the chest, or holding objects; squatting figurines, figurines in lie postrate, dancing figurines, those driving a carriage or playing instruments, walking or mounted ones. As far as the social positions of the figurines, there are generals, footmen, mounted soldiers, eunuches, house keepes or butlers, house maids, musicians and cabmen. In short, we have found at Yangling a perplexing host of pottery figurines of all descriptions; as these burial objects include members from nearly all walks of life, save members of the royal family itself, they offer valuable clues for further researches.

After detailed analyses and research of a multitude of pottery figurines, a lot can be inferred with regards to the making of the pottery figurines with authentic clothes, and it can be summed up as follows: the first procedure is to select suitable earth which is purified through sifting and washing. The earth is then mixed with ceramsite of suitable moisture and density; this mixture is then placed in the pre-fabricated models. The models are classified into four main shapes: that of the head, body, leg and foot. The second procedure is to stick to the part already made such lesser organs as the nose, ear and generta organ; this done, deep holes are pierced in the nose, ear and anus. In order to avoid close resemblance of the thousands of pottery figurines, the artisans gave an artistic touch on the face of these figurines by means of pinching, sculpturing and carving so that the figurines cast in the same model vary in likeness and posture. As the next move, the various parts of the figurines are stuck together to assume the human form. The third procedure is heating: the earthenware models are heated in the kilns so that they become hard ceramic. The forth procedure is colouring. The heated pottery figurines are coloured as in accords to the colour of the corresponding parts of the body. For instance, the figurine's hair, brows, eyes and beards are coloured dark brown while the face and body in orange. What merits our attention is when colouring the figurines, the artisans gave more artistic elaborations by adding strokes on the face of the figures so that they appear more vivid and true to life. The fifth procedure is re-heating. The coloured figures are subject to heat treatment for the second time so that the colours will more closely adhere to the body of figurines. The sixth procedure is that of carving. Along with the making of pottery bodies, wooden arms and hands are also made with movable joints. The seventh procedure is assembling. The wooden arms and hands that have been carved are assembled to the shoulders of the pottery figurines through the two holes left at the left and right shoulders. This done, a pottery figurine is basicly finished. What remains of the work is to clothe and equip these pottery figurines according to their need. For instance, those in the accompanying pits in the south and north areas are designated for military arrays. So there is a great demand of pottery warriors in these pits which the artisans made by clothing the earthenware figures, adding armour plates and arming them with shields and tridents. So what you see is a column of gallant warriors which are then placed in the accompanying pits according to the prescribed military rites.

As compared with the pottery figurines in authentic clothes, those with clothes in high relief found in the architectural ruins and accompanying tombs are relatively simple in artisanship. Mostly they underwent such steps as modeling, sculpturing, heating and colouring but without carving and assembling. Ironically, in the course of two thousand years the elaborate clothes and wooden arms of the superior form of figurines have all rotted away revealing the "ugly" naked body while those figurines of those inferior type with sculptured clothes in high relief are still true to their original form. From these pottery figurines of the Han period we can not only appreciate the beauty of human forms but also enjoy some glimpses at the garments used during the great reign of Wendi and Jingdi.

Buried under the earth for more than two thousand years, the wooden arms and coloured apparel of the clad pottery figurines, as mentioned already, have mostly decayed. But with careful observation and meticulous clearing on the part of the archaeologists, the garments are brought to light clear and vivid. Basing on these remnant cloth and with reference to the apparel in high relief, it is not difficult to reconstruct the basics of the clothes of the pottery figurines at Yingling.

1. Hair-do: The hair on the heads of the pottery figurines is, without exception, neatly combed; it is either worn in a cone, or in an oval, or in a bun, or in some other styles.

(1) Hair worn in a the shape of a cone. The hair is combed back and tied in a bun at its end. This dangling style hairdo was dominant among women in the Qin and Han periods. The style is so named because it resembles a cone. The originally clothed but presently naked female pottery figurines at Yangling all wear their hair in this style. A few male warrior figurines also wear their hair like this. As recorded in the "Biography of Lu Jia" in *The History of the Han*, "when Lu Jia arrived, Zhao Tuo wearing his hair in a cone-shaped fashion came to meet him." Fu Jian who gives the explanatory note to the quotation has this to say: "Tying hair in a cone is the fashion of the hairdo of soldiers of the time." This shows that some armymen at that time wore their hair in the above mentioned fashion.

(2) Pony tail style. When combing the hair, a parting is left in the middle of the hair which is separated into two parts on the forehead; the hair is then tied on the back of the neck with a bun dangling on the back. A strand of hair comes out of the bun dangling on one side. This style of hairdo which was an elaborate fashion began in the Han and was dominant throughout the Han period. After the Eastern Han, few people did their hair like that; and the style nearly disappeared in the Wei and Jing periods. The painted female pottery figurines unearthed at No. 130 tomb in the accompanying graveyard all wear their hair in this fashion.

(3) Tying the hair in an oval: the unearthed figurines of male warriors and servants and some mounted soldiers all have their hair tied at the back of the head in an oval. The oval shaped hair fashion can be divided into two types: that in a pig-tail style and that without plaits. The first type, i.e., the pig-tail style can be subdivided into two patterns: the first type is to cluster all the hair behind the back of the head in a broad pig-tail which is then folded upward behind the back of the head; the upper part of the folded plait is on the same level with the top of the head while the plait of other figurines is slightly higher than the top of the head; a small hair bun is tied at the end of this plait with a hair pin. Another style is to leave a parting when combing the hair so that the hair is divided into two parts; each part of the hair is then made into six or seven small plaits which are folded upward and clustered together behind the back of the head. A hair-pin is inserted in the cluster of the hair so as to fix it at the back of the head. This kind of hairdo is found on the heads of mounted soldiers' figurines unearthed in the accompanying burial pits in the south area. It is relatively simpler to tie the hair in a bun without hair-plaits. What they did was to comb all the hair to the back of the head; this done, the cluster of hair is folded with the back side dangling on the back of the head. The part of the hair which is higher than the top of the head is tied in a oval which is fixed with a hair-pin.

(4) Tying the hair in a bun. Among the mounted figurines unearthed in the accompanying pits in the south area, there are some with their cheek-bones sticking out. The hairdo of the these figurines is also peculiar. There are not any hair plaits on their heads; what you see is only a strand of hair in a bun behind their heads. To tie the hair like this, you have to comb your hair neatly and let it hang behind the head in a ring; the rest of the hair is inserted in the ring in a circle. The end of this braid of hair is pressed behind the hair stuffed in the ring. We do not know exactly the name of the hairdo; but since it is like a bun we might as well call it the bun style hairdo.

2. The style of hats: traces of remnant silk were found round the heads of many pottery figurines in the accompanying burial pits of the south area. We would not be in great error to say that some of the pottery figurines used to have hats on. As most of the hats had rotted away with the passage of time, we can not tell for certain what these hats were like. However, we can reconstruct one kind of hat they wore by availing ourselves of the traces of the silk around the heads of two pottery figures unearthed in the No. 20 burial pit. The hair ornaments of these two pottery figurines are relatively well preserved. We found that between the temples and the neck-bone was a red painted area about two c.m. wide and very brightly colored. From the pattern of the traces on the color zone we guess it is the silk remnant which is perhaps a kind of ribbon which is to tie the hair. According to "the Biography of Zhou Bo" in *The History of the Han,* Empress Dowager Bao did Wendi's hair with a ribbon"; and this is explained by Yin Xun who provides this foot note: That sort of ornament is in fact a kind of ribbon. In the majority of cases, ancient people wore their hair long and, after combing it, they tied the hair with a cloth ribbon which had similar functions as the hair ribbons used by modern women.

The hats found on the heads of the

pottery figurines have a round top with a brim narrower in the front and broad in the rear; at each side of the brim hangs a long sash. The hats are shaped like an inverted dust-pan. The texture of the hats, mostly of cloth, is fine but loosely woven with very tiny holes. This type of hat is very much like a cap used in ancient times called bian. As recorded in "Hats and Caps" in *A Dictionary for Special Terms,* "*bian* is like clasped hands". According to the explanation of "Costumes and Garments" in *The Continuation of the History of the Han, bian* is "like an inverted mug; it is high and broad in the front but low and narrow at the back." From the above descriptions and explanations it is not difficult to see that the ancient cap *bian* resembles two clasped hands, or an inverted mug with a holder. Beginning from the Qin period, warriors in China had been wearing *bian*. In "The Costumes" in T*he Rites of the Zho*u it is recorded: "*Bian* is commonly used in the military." The three thousand or so pottery warriors unearthed from Yangjiawan all wear *bian*, similar to their counterparts at Yangling.

3. Clothes: As a social custom, the Han people liked to wear garments hanging long. This preference is clearly born out in the attire of the pottery figures unearthed at Yangling. The garments as seen in the clothes sculptured in high relief are clear and simple and they can be summed up as follows:

(1) The upper part of the garment is attached to its lower part with a sewn seam at the joint near the waist.

(2) The collar of the garment is shaped in a square with folds.

(3) The sleeves are extended by attaching another part which forms an angle with the root sleeve; when the clothes are put on, the sleeves can be flung to the back so that the underwears will not be exposed. These, again, are characteristics of long clothes.

The long gown, also known as the "deep gown", originated in the Spring and Autumn period, and they are prevalent in the Warring States and the Western Han periods. All the people irrespective of gender and their social position could wear it. It is called "deep gown" because of its being broad and long. The pottery figurines with sculptured clothes on high relief unearthed at Yangling from all walks of life and irrespective of sex all wear deep gown. This speaks eloquently of the prevalence of the deep gowns.

The clothes on the clad pottery figurines have, as indicated above, mostly rotted away and are beyond recognition. As far as the clad figurines unearthed in the accompanying burial pits in the south area are concerned, these were warriors who needed to fight in battles and conduct military marches. It would not be realistic for these warriors to wear deep gowns or long robes which are long and broad on the sleeves and which have no opening on the chest; for sure that would make it difficult for the warriors in this attire to engage in military activities. Most of the warrior figurines with sculptured clothes unearthed in the mausoleum of Emperor Qin-shi-huang-di (the First Emperor of All China) and those in the Han tomb at Yangjiawan wear clothes called *Changru* that reach the knees. The main difference between *Changru* and the long gown is that of the length of the clothes. While the deep gown reaches the feet, *Changru* reaches only the knees. Judging by the cloth remains of the pottery figurines unearthed in the accompanying burial pits in the south area, we can tell that the warrior figurines of Yingling also wear their garments reaching their knees only. This kind of clothes are relatively short with narrower sleeves making it easy for movement and for doing manual labor. It is therefore reasonable to assume that the clothes the originally clad figurines wore are a kind of *Changru*.

On the lower legs of most of the warrior figurines we have found some reddish cloth showing traces of wrapping; obviously it is a sort of puttee. The puttee of the Han armymen is made of a big cloth with bands at the four corners. What the warriors did was first to rap it on the lag and then wind it downward assuming the shape of the English letter "z"; this done, the puttee is fast wrapped on the lag. *Shiming* (or *Denoting Special Terms,* an ancient dictionary) has this to say: "*Fu*, also referred to as *Xingfu* is a sort of puttee for wrapping the leg." This sort of leg wrapping is comparable to the puttee of the modern armyman. The warrior figurines unearthed in the Yangjiawan and those found in the First Emperor's mausoleum wear similar puttees. This also shows the sort of puttee was popular in the Qin and Han periods.

4. Armour plates. A multitude of warrior figurines in armour plates were found in the accompanying burial pits in the south area. As they are made of leather, most of the plates had rotted away when they were unearthed. What remained of the armour plates were traces of brown and black substances. It is reasonable to infer after the plates were cleared out that they assume the shape of a square with each side measuring two centimeters. We found, as we examined the plates, two small holes in the middle of each side for joining the adjacent plates with threads. The plates on the collar are arranged with one overlapping the other either from the upper part to the lower part, or from left to right. Each set of armour plates, slightly shorter than *Changru*, is comprised of two parts, the upper part and the lower. The armour plates on the chest are made of six tiers overlapping one another and joined with ropes. The lower part of the

plates on the chest was shaped like a trumpet with the opening at the bottom; there are four tiers overlapping one another all from left to right. The arrangement of the plates on the back is just the opposite from those on the chest. There are only two tiers of plates covering the arms.[31] As these plates are shaped like bamboo slits, they are referred to as "slits" in ancient documents. The image of the pottery figurines in armour plates of the Han period is the most characteristic of those found at the Han tomb at Yangjiawan. Most of the pottery warriors found there wear armour plates. Some figurines are just covered on the chest and back while some others have additional plates covering their arms and lower part of their waist.[32] In terms of the time period and nature of the burial pit, the one at Yingjiawan is similar to that of the south area at Yingling. From what we can see when clearing these relics, the armour plates found on the warriors in these two different pits should fall to the same type.

5. Shoes. The people in the Qin and Han periods wore many different kinds of shoes including *li, xi, ju,* sandals and boots. On formal occasions, however, they only wore *li*. From the pottery figurines with sculptured clothes unearthed at Yangling, we can tell that the shoes they wore are a kind of *li*. Regrettably, there are not any traces of shoes worn on the originally clothed figurines there; but judging by the attire of these figurines it is reasonable to infer that the kind of shoes these wore are *li* also. The earthenware figurines unearthed at Yanjiawan which are very similar to those from Yangling, as we already know, wear four kinds of shoes: straw sandals called *mang*, square shaped *li* with a sharp pointed tip, shallow shoes with a round opening and boots with embroideries.[33] It is safe to infer that the originally clad earthenware figurines at Yangling also wore these types of shoes. Generally, most warriors wore straw sandals while cavalrymen wore shallow shoes with a round opening. The other two types of shoes were less popular.

Judging by the style and workmanship of the pottery figurines, we can tell for certain that those found at Yangling were the outcome of the fusion of two different cultures and burial systems. The making and the outer appearance of the pottery figures with sculptured clothes found at Yangling are akin to their counterparts the Terri Cotta Warriors found near the First Emperor's (Qin-shi-huang-di's)tomb, while the "deep clothes" worn by most pottery figurines at Yangling are, beyond a shadow of a doubt, characteristic of the Chu culture (Chu being a kingdom in southern China prior to China's unification by the Qing regime.)

The prolonged sleeves and the outer silk garments on the originally clad figurines differ noticeably from the attire of those Terri Cotta Warriors of the Qin; for this kind of clothes are only seen on the figurines of the Chu kingdom. We have seen clothes worn on the Chu wooden figurines at Yuhuatai of Jialing, Hubei province, and in some Chu tombs in Changsha, Hunan province. This fashion of clothes such as have been found in the Western Han tombs were inherited by the Han people who happened to live in areas which had originally been the realm of the kingdom of Chu. Incidentally, about a generation ago an early Han tomb at Mawangdui, Hunan province was opened, in which were unearthed two male figurines with clothes and hats on, ten clothed figurines of house maids and eight clothed figurines of musicians, all of which are made of wood. The figurines are crudely carved and without limbs, but they are clad in thin silk.[34] It is safe to infer, therefore, that the making of the nude pottery figurines that were originally clothed had been strongly influenced by the Chu culture.

The earthenware animal figurines at Yangling mainly include horses, cows, oxen, sheep, pigs and chickens. The making of these animal figures was very elaborate: it included such processes as modelling, sculpturing, heating and colouring as was the case with the making of the clothed human figurines. In addition, more meticulous work such as carving and assembling was also employed, too. (The wooden horns and tails of cows, sheep and horses, for instance, were assembled afterwards).

There is a bewildering host of pottery animal figurines unearthed at Yangling which are lively and true to life. The pottery cows, as you can see, are heavily built with strong muscular limbs and short and stout necks, stretched out ears and sticking out eyes, all of which show their strength, stubborness and honesty. The pottery sheep, on the other hand, have rounded bodies, thin limbs, sticking out ears and drooping beard, slightly open mouths, big hips and dangling tails. The pottery goats, too, have rounded bodies; but with their straight legs like pillars and their ears and little tails pointed upward, they look mild and lovely. The pottery pigs have fat and meaty bodies, short legs; their bellies with two rows of nipples hang low; their necks are short and thick; their ears are big and mouths long, assuming a funny look. As you see in the pit, there are two kinds of pottery dogs—the wolf-hounds and the domestic dogs. The former have sticking out ears and piecing eyes looking forward; their mouths are thin and a bit long, and their cheeks slightly bulge. Their necks are short and bodies strong. They have strong limbs and tails hanging low. The latter, i.e., the domestic dogs, on the other hand, have rounded bodies with ears pointing upward and eyes sticking out; their mouths are short and thick and tails curled upward. Both kinds of dogs are supurbly modeled and elegantly sculptured; they give the viewer a formidable forbearance. The pottery chickens, both roosters and hens, are very colourfully painted throughout the body. The roosters have high raised heads, shot-out tails, long beaks and small eyes; their high cockscombs are painted red while their feathers are painted in black, red, and yellow. The hens have slightly smaller bodies and shorter tails; their heads, too, are raised high but without cockscombs. Both roosters and hens, alike in spirit and image to those in real life, are vividly sculptured, which eloquently speak of the ingenious workmanship of our ancient artisans. In terms of number and artisanship, the animal figurines unearthed at Yangling have no parallel in history.[35]

The pottery figurines at Yangling, both humans and animals, are the embodiment of the Western Han society that covers such realms as politics, economy, military and culture; and they provide us with valuable information for the study, research and rare insights for a good grasp of the Western Han history. Moreover, they are of great importance in the study of art history. From the preliminary studies we have hitherto conducted, we can tell for certain that while on one hand the Yangling pottery figurines have inherited such artistic traditions of the Terri Cotta Warriors of the Qin period as "realistic depicting", "observing special features in modelling", "emphasis on grace and simplicity", " skillful artisanship", "artistic combination of painting and sculpturing" and "varied artistic forms and multi-processes in the making of the figurines",[(36)] they have, on the other hand, discarded the stiff and prosaic genre of the earlier periods to absorb the pith of model making of the Chu people. In so doing, the manufacturing of the Yangling burial figurines gave a prodigious birth of a brand new art form which includes "simplistic and freehand expression of art", "natural combination of painting, sculpturing, carving, and colouring", "likeness in producing art work"and"romanticism", thus creating a new art genre which manifests itself in the numerous meticulously yet lively produced sculptures we are beholding and pushing the development of China's ancient carving and sculpturing to a new high.

(Translated by Zhang Yalun, professor of the English Department, Xi'an Foreign Language University, Xi'an,China)

Notes

1. "The Biography of King Xiaojing", *The Historical Records (Shiji)*.

2. "The Biography of Jingdi", The *History of the Han*.

3. The "Empress's Relatives", *The History of the Han*.

4. Qin Zhongxing. "Findings in the Convicts' Graves Near Han Yangling," *Archaeology*, Vol. 12, 1976.

5. Wang Peizhong, Zhang Zipo and Sun Derun. "A Brief Account of the Investigations of Emperor Jingdi's Mausoleum at Han Yangling," *Archaeology and Cultural Relics,* Vol. 1, 1980.

6. Liu Qingzhu and Li Yufang. "Investigations and Research of the Mausoleums of the Western Han," *The Journal of Cultural Relics and Records,* Vol. 6, 1982. Also from *The Eleven Mausoleums of the Western Han,* Shaanxi People's Press, July, 1987.

7. The Archaeological Team of Han Yangling under Shaanxi Provincial Archaeological Research Institute. "Bulletin No. 1 About the Accompanying Burial Pit in the South Area of Emperor Jingdi's Mausoleum at Yangling." *Cultural Relics* Vol. 4, 1992. Also in "Bulletin No 2," by the same author, Cultural relics, vol. 4, 1994; and in "The Coloured Pottery Figurines at Han Yangling in China," Shaanxi Tourism Press, 1992.

8. Jiao Nanfeng, Wang Baoping, Ma Yongying, Li Gang and others. "The Accompanying Burial Graveyards Found at Emperor Han Jingdi's Mauloseum at Yangling," *Journal for China's Cultural Relics,* Nov. 14, 1999; also in "Rare Cultural Relics discovered in the Numerous Accompanying Pits at Han Yangling," *Journal for China's Cultural Relics,* Nov. 28, 1999.

9. The Archaeological Team of Han Yangling under Shaanxi Provincial Archaeological Research Institute. "New Discoveries at Emperor Han Jingdi's Mausoleum at Yangling," Wenbo, Vol. 6, 1999.

10. Jiao Nanfeng, Wang Baoping, Ma Yongying, Li Gang and others. "Rare Cultural Relics Discovered in the Numerous Accompanying Pits at Han Yangling," *Journal for China's Cultural Relics,* Nov. 28, 1999.

11.Due to incomplete excavations, the pertinent data are still kept at the Archaeological Team of Han Yangling.

12. Ibid.

13. Ibid.

14. Same as Note 10.

15. Same as Note 9.

16. "The Coloured Pottery Figurines at Han Yangling in China," Shaanxi Tourism Press, 1992.

17. Dong Hongwen and others. "Surveying and Research of the Pelorus at Yangling," *Information on Surveying and Mapping,* Vol. 6, 1995.

18. Jiao Nanfeng. "The Capital in the Han Period and Excavations in and Researches into the Emperors' Mausoleums."—to be published.

19. Qin Zhongxing. "Findings in the Convicts' Graves Near Han Yangling,

" Archaeology, Vol. 12, 1976.

20. "A Chart of the Civil Officials who Rendered Outstanding Service, under Emperors Gaozu and Huidi, Empress Lu (Widow of Gaozu) and Emperor Wendi," *The History of the Han.*

21. Jiao Nanfeng, Wang Baoping, Ma Yongying, Li Gang and others. "The Accompanying Burial Graveyards Found at Emperor Han Jingdi's Mauloseum at Yangling," *Journal for China's Cultural Relics,* Nov. 14, 1999.

22.Jiao Nanfeng and Ma Yongying. "The Emperors' Mausoleums of the Western Han Do not Follow the System of the Tomb of King Zhou Mu," Wenbo, Vol. 5, 1999.

23. Zhao Huacheng. "The Historical Trail: from the Common Cemetary System of the Shang and the Zhou to the Independent Mausoleum System of the Qin and the Han,"*Bulletin Information about Ancient Civilization,* (Excerpts) Vol. 6, 2000.

24. Jiao Nanfeng. "The Capital in the Han Period and Excavations in and Researches into the Emperors' Mausoleums."—to be published.

25. Sun Ji. Illustrated Information on the Material Aspects of the Han Culture: the Rostrum and Its Gates, the Cultural Relics Press, 1991.

26. *The Stone Rostrums of the Han Period in Sichuan Province, by the Cultural Bureau of Chongqing and the Museum of Chongqing,* the Cultural Relics Press, 1992.

27. Jiao Nanfeng. "Walls and Rostrums in the Mausoleums of the Han Period," Journal for China's Cultural Relics, Nov. 30, 1999.

28. Li Gang. "A Weiqi (go) Chessboard Found at Han Yangling," *Journal for China's Cultural Relics,* Dec. 5, 1999.

29. Wang Xueli. "The Historical Significance of the Wooden Arms in the Clothed Pottery Figurines," Wenbo, Vol. 6, 1997.

30. Pertinent data kept in the Yangling Archaeological Team.

31. The Archaeological Team of Han Yangling under Shaanxi Provincial Archaeological Research Institute. "Bulletin No. 2 on the Accompanying Burial Pit in the South Area of Emperor Jingdi's Mausoleum at Yangling." *Cultural Relics*, Vol. 4, 1994.

32. Yang Bingli and Shi Yukuan. *The Three Thousand Colour Painted Pottery Figurines of the Western Han,* Shaanxi Fine Art Press, 1996.

33. Ibid.

34.*Han Tomb No. One at Mawangdui, Changsha,* Cultural Press, 1973.

35. Wang Baoping. "Exquisite Sculptures of Animals of the Han, Journal for China's Relics," Nov. 30, 1999.

36. *Yuan Zhongyi. A Research into the Terri Cotta Warriors in Emperor Qin-shi-huang-di's Mausoleum,* the Cultural Relics Press, 1990.

漢陽陵

はじめに

90年代以来、陝西省考古学研究所は漢景帝陽陵で、大規模な考古学的調査・探査・発掘を行い、注目される多くの成果を上げた。そして1999年10月1日、漢陽陵考古陳列館が正式に開館したのである。その状況を多くの専門家に理解してもらいたく、漢陵における考古学的調査を更に進め、また多くの旅行者に「文景の治」の風格を十分理解して頂く、我々は特にこの小冊子をもって読者に紹介したい。

1，陽陵の歴史地理の状況

漢景帝は名を劉啓といい、前漢第４代目の皇帝である。景帝は漢恵帝７年(紀元前188年)に生まれ、32歳の時に即位した。在位は17年で、歴史発展の潮流に乗って“黄老の術”を引継いで奉り、国内において.“無爲而治”“與民休息”を実行し、“七国の乱”を平定した。また対外においては「和親匈奴」を持って国家の安定を維持すると共に、中央集権統治を強化し、経済発展を促進させるなど漢文帝年間の発展を基礎に、明朗な政治、国家の安定、経済の繁栄、国民の裕福さを得、中国封建社会発展史上第一の頂点を形成したのである。

陽陵は漢景帝と王皇后の同墓不同穴の合葬陵園である。漢景帝前元四年(紀元前153年)“更以弋陽爲陽陵”[1]として寿陵の造営を開始し、“後元三年(紀元前141年),甲子……帝崩於未央宮。二月癸酉，葬陽陵”[2]“孝景王皇后，武帝母也。……後景帝十五歲，元朔三年(紀元前126年)崩，合葬陽陵。”[3]としたのである。

陽陵は現在の陝西省咸陽市渭城区正陽鎮張家湾に位置し、後溝村北の咸陽原上で、咸陽市渭城区・涇陽県・高陵県の三県に跨る。陽陵の北には涇河が流れ、南には渭河と長安城が一望でき、東は“涇渭の会”を臨み、西は漢高祖長陵と境を接する。

2，陽陵の考古学発掘研究過程

陽陵において現代考古学的意義を持って科学的探査を開始したのは20世紀70年代からである。1972年に陝西省歴史博物館の研究者が発見、試掘をへて陽陵刑徒墓地を確定した。[4]1978年、咸陽市博物館考古学調査隊が陽陵の陵園に対して考古学的調査を行い、帝陵・皇后陵・門闕・陪葬墓の一部などで探査を行った。[5]80年代には中国社会科学院考古研究所の専門家が陽陵で全面的な調査を行い、多くの収穫を得た。[6]

1990年5月から1994年の10月にかけて、西安—咸陽国際空港専用道路の建設に伴い、陝西省考古研究所漢陵考古隊は陽陵の大規模な考古学発掘と研究を行った。約５年の努力によって、前後して従葬坑２組、建築遺跡数座を探査・発見し、またその中の南区従葬坑の部分発掘を行った。[7]南区従葬坑の配置は独特で、豊富な内容を呈し、保存状態が良く、出土陶俑など各類文物の数量も多く、1990年の全国十大考古発見の１つと称された。

1995年以来、新たに設けた陽陵考古隊は今後の研究の基礎上において重要な帝陵の配置結合及び陪葬墓園に対して大規模な調査・測量・探査・発掘を行い、陵園の全体配置の規模を更に明らかにし、帝陵の形成の大まかを把握し、大量の陪葬墓園を発見した。同時に帝陵南門闕遺跡の発掘、いくつかの中小陪葬墓の調査を行った。発掘で出土した各類文物は9300件あまりを数え重要な成果を得たのである。[8]

1999年10月1日、漢陽陵考古陳列館の建設と対外への開放は陽陵考古発掘と研究保護、開発と建設において新たな１章を開くものである。

3，陽陵考古発掘紀要

発掘研究を通して得たのは次の通りである。陽陵の陵園平面形は不規則な葫蘆形を呈し、東西長さ約6km、南北広さ約１から3kmで面積は約12km^{2}である。帝陵、皇后陵、南・北区従葬坑、刑徒墓地、陵廟など礼制建築、陪葬墓及び陽陵邑などの部分から成る。帝陵は東向きで、陵園の中部よりやや西に位置する。皇后陵、南区従葬坑、北区従葬坑、１号建築遺跡などは距離を等しくして帝陵の４角に位置する。嬪妃陪葬墓区と羅盤石遺跡は帝陵の南北両側に位置し、左右対称となる。刑徒墓地及び３基の建築遺跡は帝陵の西側南北１列に配列されている。陪葬墓園は帝陵の東側の司馬道の両側に碁盤上に分布している。そのため陽陵邑は帝陵の東端に設置された。陵園全体は帝陵を中心とし、４隅を取り囲み、南北は対称で、東西は相連なり、配置は規制され、結合は厳格で、唯我独尊の皇家意識と厳格な等級観念を明確にしている。

帝陵陵園の平面は正方形を呈し、辺長は417.5—418mである。４辺には夯土の壁が囲み、寛さ3.00－3.50mである。４辺の壁の中部には「三出」門闕が、４隅には無角楼などの建築遺跡が存在する。陵園中部は封土を積み、覆斗形を呈し、底辺から上に行くほど小さくなり、底部の辺長は167.5－168.5m、高さは32.28mである。帝陵は「亜」字形をなし、東を向く。

帝陵封土以外に、４条の墓道の両側で従葬坑が86座探査発見されており、東側に21座、北側に21座、西側に20座、南側に19座存在する。東西両側の坑は東西方向に、南北両側の坑は南北方向を向き、陵園の東北角の５座は南北１列に配される。坑の寛さは3－4mで、最長の坑は100mを越え、最短の坑は4mほどしかない。坑の深さは3m程で、坑底部から現地表面まで8－14mある。探査資料から、従葬坑内には騎兵、歩兵、動物などの各陶俑、陶、銅、漆器などの生活用具、兵器、車両、車馬具などがあることがわかっている。[9]

1998年から1999年、我々は帝陵東側の11号、13号、19号などの従葬坑で局部試掘を行った。第13号坑は竪穴式長条形土坑で、長さ92m、寛さ3m、深さ３mで坑底部から地表までの距離は8mである。坑は地下隧道式の構築物を設けている。その構築方法はまず地面をならし、0.6—0.7mの高さで幾層かの土盛りをし、更に盛り土を約３m、夯土・黒土、更に生土約1.7m掘る。更に整地した後、坑底部両側に長条形の木材を並べ、その上に横木を並べる。その底板の両側に柱を立て、柱の間を横木で埋め、その上に桁木を渡し、桁木の上を藁などで多い、その上部の高さを地面と同一にし、隧道式の空間を形成する。その後陪葬品を配置し、最後に木材で門を塞ぐ。従葬坑の上部には厚さ約3.5－６mの五花夯土が堆積し、その上は近代堆積層と耕土層である。第11号坑の長さは74m、第19号坑は長さ20m、その寛さ、深さ、機構、地層などは第13号坑と同じかそれに近い。

13号坑の試掘部分は長さ22mで、上部棚部調査の後、帝陵に向かって配列が密集した動物陶俑群が現れ、その種類によって４区に分けることが出来る。第１区間は坑の東部で長さ約7m、235件の彩陶山羊が黒色と赤色に分けられていた。第２区間は第１区間の西側に位置し、長さが約７m、彩色陶犬が458体置かれていた。雄雌あり、また種類から狼犬と家犬の２つに分けられる。顔の色は黄色、白、黒、灰、橙紅色の５色に分けられ、彩色陶犬の口と鼻の部分にはまた紅色が塗られていた。第３，４区間は第２区間の西側で長さは約８mである。北半部が第３区間で、６列３３体の彩色陶綿羊が置かれており、顔の色が黒と橙紅色に分けられる。第３区間の南側に位置する第４区間からは２列54体の子豚が出土した。黒と白の２色に分けられ、子豚は耳が立ち、口は長く、尾が小さく、生き生きとしており、かわいらしい。この層の動物の下にはなお木板で区切られ、木板の下には彩色陶動物俑があった。[10]

第11号坑はその中部の24m²を試掘し、帝陵を背にし東門を向いた騎兵４列と木車２列を発見し、木車を中心に騎兵が両側に列をなしていた。騎兵俑は26体、彩色木馬17体、木車４両、銅鉄質兵器、車馬器100あまりが出土した。[11]

第19号坑は面積約12m²を試掘し、木馬４体、木車１両、武士俑20余体、動物俑10余体、銅鉄質兵器、車馬器及び陶器など30点あまりが出土した。その配列順序は木馬を前にし、木車が中央、武士俑がその両側を守り、動物俑と陶器などは車の後方両側に置かれていた。[12]

この他、第16号、第18号坑の上部の盗掘坑中から“太官之印”、宦者俑等が出土し、これらの従葬坑の性質を考えるのに重要なヒントを与えてくれた。[13]

陽陵帝陵南闕門遺跡は陵園南部の真ん中に位置し、帝陵封土から120ｍの距離で、1997年3月から６月に発掘を行った。合わせて10×10ｍのグリッドを56カ所、実際の調査面積は3100m²で、大型建築遺跡を１組２基発見し、板瓦、瓦当、脊獣、囲碁盤、博具盤、鉄夯頭等の遺物583が出土した。

南闕門遺跡は１組２基の三出闕が連なる構成で、三出闕の平面形は大から次第に小さくなる三つの長方形の組み合わせである。闕門の中間には中央門道、その両側に東西内外の４塾、塾の外側に主闕台、主闕台の外側に副闕台がある。主、副闕台は共に版築で造られ、 土外壁には厚さ約1－2cmの藁泥を塗り、その外側に白灰面を施し、最後に朱を塗る。塾、主闕台、副闕台の周囲には回廊が巡る。回廊の地面には方磚が敷かれる。回廊の外側は鵝卵石を敷いて散水し、内高外低で魚脊形を為す。全ての建築は位置は整い、左右対称で、結合は合理的で、規模が大きく、保存も良好で、非常にまれな漢代建築である。[14]

南闕門遺跡の塾と主、副闕台は基礎版築の色が明らかに異なり、塾は黄褐色、主、副闕台は紅褐色を呈しており、明らかに１回の築造ではない。その両部分を結ぶ基礎連結の版築は、主、副闕台に近い側で草泥、白灰面と朱色を施しているが、主、副闕台の年代はやや早く、塾は少し遅れて建てられたものである。主、副闕台の年代は陽陵が建造されるのと同期、即ち漢景帝年間と思われる。《漢書》に、漢武帝元鼎三年(紀元前114年)“正月戊子、陽陵園火”の記載がある。我々は塾の建築年代は、この火災の後すぐではないかと推測している。言い換えると、塾の建築年代は武帝年間になる。この推測は、遺跡柱洞中から出土した五銖銭と、早晩両期の板瓦や筒瓦、瓦当等建築材料の時期が異なることと一致する。

皇后陵陵園の平面は正方形で、辺長さ347.5－350ｍである。四辺は版築の壁が巡り、その壁の中央には門が、四隅には無角楼の類の建築遺跡が設けられる。封土は陵園の中部に位置し、覆斗形を為し、上小底大で底辺長約160ｍ、高さ26.49ｍである。皇后陵の形成も亜字形を為し、東向きである。東西南北には各一本の墓道があり、東側が最長最寛である。封土の外側には従葬坑も巡っている。[15]

南区従葬坑は帝陵東南、皇后陵の真南に位置する。96000m² を占め、14行24本の従葬坑が東西に配列され、平面形は長方形と"中"字形の２類あり、南北に向いている。長さは25－291ｍで、寛さは４ｍ、行の距離は20ｍ程である。北区従葬坑は帝陵の西北に位置し、その面積、坑数、行数、配列は南区と同じである。90年から97年に前後して南区の14の坑に対して部分試掘や全体発掘を行い、これらの坑中から配列の密集した武士俑群、糧食を入れた貯蔵庫、牛や羊、豚、犬、鶏などの陶質動物及び組を成す陶、鉄、銅質の生活用具を発見し、漢代の軍旅の情景、そして西漢時期の"南軍"、"北軍"の関係を明らかにした。[16]

羅経石遺跡は帝陵の東南に位置する。ここの地形は隆起しており、外形は波状になっている。考古探査から、遺跡の平面は方形に近く、辺長さ260ｍで、外側には壕溝が巡っている。遺跡の中心部分の最高点に方形巨石が１塊置かれており、当地の人は"羅経石"と呼んでいる。その巨石は黒雲母花崗岩に加工が成されており、南北長183cm、東西寛180cm、厚さ40cmである。石版の上部は直径140cmの円盤状に加工され、その表面には十字の溝があり、その寛さ・深さ共約2.3cmで、正南北方向を示している。[17]研究から、その巨石は陽陵建造の水平の標準で、高度を測り方位を指し示すためのもので、目下世界最古の測量標準石である。遺跡の試掘中に、遺跡中部から１基の版築土台が発見され、主体建築の基台と思われる。その遺跡の辺は長さ54ｍ、毎辺３つの門があり、合わせて12の門が存在する。四周は地面に磚が敷かれ、卵石で散水し、四神空心磚及び瓦片堆積層などの遺跡や遺物が存在する。この建築遺跡の地形は高く、配置は整い、規模が非常に大きいことから陽陵陵園中最も重要な礼制建築の一つであると思われる。[18]

刑徒墓地は帝陵の西北約1.5kmに位置し、その面積は８万m²にも及び、70年代初の発見からここに葬られた刑徒の数は１万以上と推算される。72年に発掘した29基の墓葬からは35体の人骨が発見され、その墓送配列は無秩序で、骨は散乱し、相互に折り重なり合い、埋葬はいい加減で、陪葬品もない。骨格上に多くに"鉗"や"鈦"等の鉄製刑具が填められ、いくつかには明らかな切断痕跡も認められる。[19]

帝陵陵園と皇后陵陵園内部、帝陵西部と北部、南区従葬坑の南部からは大量の建築遺跡が発見され、その詳細には更なる探査や発掘が待たれる。

陪葬墓園区は、西端が帝陵から東に1100ｍのところで、東は馬家湾郷米家崖村の付近までである。全長2350ｍで、約3.5km² を占める。その東と西の両端には南北に長い１本の壕溝があり、陪葬墓葬区東西の境界線となっており、中部は陪葬墓葬区の司馬道が横に貫き、数量の多い陪葬墓園がその両側に配列されている。目下探査によって壕溝で隔てられた陪葬墓園16列107基が発見されている。墓園内には数量の異なる墓葬と陪葬坑等がある。これらの墓園は東西に排を成し、南北に列をなし、碁盤状に分布している。すでに5000余基の墓葬が明らかとなり、その中の337基で調査が行われ、合わせて各類文物5516件が出土した。その内分けは鍾、鈁、罐、倉、灶、鼎、鉢等の陶器1283件、鍾、鈁、鏡、帯鈎、車馬器、弩機、印章、小銅飾等を主とした銅器772件、半両、五銖、大泉五十、小泉直一等各類銅銭2923枚、鉄剣、鉄斧、鉄灯、環首刀等鉄器212件、玉圭、玉含、玉蝉、玉塞等の小型玉器54件、骨器、貝製品、石器、漆器等102件である。

これらの墓園の配置と墓葬の形成及び出土遺物の分析から、上述の墓園を早、中、晩の３期に分けることが出来る。

早期墓園は30期である。司馬道の両側に各２列、平面形は多くが東西向きの長方形か方形に近い。１基の墓園には１から５基の墓葬があり、主墓は甲字形を呈し、傍らには一般的に従葬坑が存在する。司馬道の南側の墓園の主墓は墓道を北側に向け、司馬道北側の墓園の墓主は墓道を南に向ける。この区の墓園中で発掘調査を行った漢墓は６０基で、出土文物は1652件である。その中の司馬道南第１列97YPIGYM130から"周応"の銅印が出土した。《漢書》等の関係史籍から、漢景帝時に"周応"が２人いたことが証明され、１人は西漢初年　の子供で景帝の時に鄲侯に封じられ、死後諡を康侯といった。もう１人は高景侯周成の孫で、"孝景中元年"にその祖の縄侯に封じられた。言い換えれば、97YPIGYM130の墓主は鄲侯周応か縄侯周応[20]ということになる。この他、司馬道南第１列97YPIGYM144では鍾、鈁、盆等の銅器が数件出土し、その中には"般邑家銅鍾容十斗重卅五斤第二家工造"の４行17文字の銘文が刻まれた銅鍾があった。"般邑家"は"陽信家"と同じで、ある諸侯や公主の封号である。"般邑"(侯、公主)は文献記載にはない。M130と"般邑"の推定や、史書の丞相李蔡、蘇建の陽陵における陪葬に関係のある記載などの結合から、この期の墓園の墓主は諸侯や公主などの皇親国戚、朝廷顕貴、郡国貴族であると思われる。言い換えれば、この区の墓園は陽陵の陪葬墓園なのである。この期の墓園の特徴は司馬道から近く、規模が大きく、壕溝は寛く深く、墓形は大きく、配列は順序立っており、墓主の級も比較的高い。

中期墓園は55期で、早期墓園の南北両側に位置し、早期墓園との間には10mほどの間隔がある。配置は比較的整い、配列もそろっている。墓園の平面の多くが方形で、門道は多くが北向きで、それぞれの墓園内には建築遺跡や陶窯が存在する。墓園東西には真っ直ぐに伸びた壕溝があり、明らかに1度の測量により位置を決め、建造されたもので、南北向きの壕溝の多くも一直線に伸びる。墓園内の墓葬は小型と中型が主で、多くは一定しない。この区の墓園中で発掘調査した漢墓は120余基で、出土文物は1850件あまりである。中期墓園の特徴は、司馬道からの距離がやや遠く、配置は比較的整い、壕溝は狭く、墓総数量が多く、面積が異なり、大形墓園内に小形墓園を内包する現象も見られる。

晩期墓園は合わせて22期が発見され、中期墓園の南北両側に位置する。中期墓園との間には約10mほどの間隔がある。墓園の平面形は方形、長方形で面積は不統一で大形墓園内に小形墓園を内包する現象も見られる。壕溝は更に狭く、浅くなる。墓園内の墓葬は非常に多く、方向は一定せず、配列規律も不鮮明で、年代差の重複関係も見られる。墓葬形成の種類も多く、磚室墓が前期より増加する。この区の墓園中で発掘調査した漢墓は100基あまりで、出土文物は1800件ほどである。早、中期と比べて晩期墓園は司馬道からの距離が最も遠く、配置は比較的整い、壕溝が狭く浅く、墓葬数量が多く、配列に企画性が欠け、墓主は比較的低い級である。

文献記載、墓園配置、墓葬形成と出土器物の分析から、漢陽陵陪葬墓園は上限が景帝年間、即ち西漢早期、その下限が東漢中期までとされる。早期墓園の時代がほぼ漢景帝が陽陵の建造を開始してから武帝年間までに相当し、中期墓園の年代が西漢中晩期、晩期墓葬の年代が西漢晩期から東漢中期となる。[21]

4，陽陵発掘の考古学意義

陵園全体配置の大まかな理解と把握は陽陵考古発掘の第1の収穫である。30年来、考古学者達は西漢11陵の陵園、帝陵、陪葬墓、従葬坑、建築遺跡などで数度の調査、測量及び試掘を行い、これらの調査、測量、試掘を通して、特にこの近年来陽陵の発掘と調査研究は西漢帝陵制度の神秘のベールを取り去り、西漢11陵の形成特徴は次第に明確になってきている。

帝陵、皇后陵が「亜」字形を呈し、東向きであることを明らかにしたことは西漢11陵の考古研究において初めてである。この発見は学会における漢陵が南向きか東向きかという長期に渡る論争を生んだ難題を基本的に解決し、漢代帝陵が昭穆制度を用いて配置されたという論点を比定し、漢代帝陵制度研究の1つの難題を解決した。[22]

帝陵園内の86本の従葬坑における探査発見と試掘などの漢陵の野外調査においては、新たな課題を提出し、帝陵制度の研究に新たな視野を開いた。これらの従葬坑の分布と坑内陪葬物品の配置は、当時の宮廷制度などと関係があることは疑いなく、そのためこれらの従葬坑の発掘と研究は、漢代の宮廷制度、帝王の生活、陪葬習俗の研究に対して重大な価値を備えている。

このたび発見した陪葬墓園の数量は非常に多く、周壕も整い、配置は企画的で、配列も順序よく並び、明らかに専心的な設計と計画に基づいている。この現象は前漢11陵の陪葬墓区の配置と形成が陽陵と同じか、またはそれに近いものであるということを暗示している。

陽陵考古発掘資料を基に西漢帝陵の発掘研究成果をまとめると、商周時期の「集中公墓制」とは異なり、西漢帝陵は秦始皇帝陵の配置結合を継承し、発展させ、「陵園独立化、陵園の規模化、設備の複雑化、効能の完全化」の重大な変革を完成させ、新たな西漢社会制度に適応した「独立陵園制」を形成し、「後の中国の2000年近い専制社会帝王陵園制度の基礎」を打ち立てたのである。[23]

目下、西漢帝陵の形成特徴としては以下のものがあげられる。

1、西漢諸陵は依山為陵、一種の「因山為蔵」の崖墓である覇陵をのぞいて、封土で築いている。封土の平面は方形で、多くは覆斗状を呈し、いくつかの陵は2層台式である。陵頂には「享堂」等の建築遺跡はない。

2、帝陵は亜字形を呈し、東向きである。東西南北の4本の墓道は東墓道を主道としている。

3、帝陵と皇后陵は「同墓不同穴」の合葬制で、帝陵を中心と、皇后陵の多くはその東北に位置する。皇后陵はより帝陵よりやや小さい。

4、西漢前期、帝陵と皇后陵は同一陵園内に位置し、一般に長方形で面積は非常に大きい。陽陵以後、帝陵と皇后陵はそれぞれの陵園を持ち、その距離は一般に450－700mの間である。平面は方形で、帝陵陵園は1辺長さ約400m、皇后陵陵園は1辺350mである。陵園の周りには土壁が巡り、それぞれの面の壁中央に門が開けられている。陽陵帝陵の4面は三出闕式で、杜陵の4面は二出台式である。

5、帝陵と皇后陵の陵園の封土と土壁の間には大量の従葬坑が存在する。帝陵と皇后陵の外側にも数量の異なる従葬坑が分布している。

6、陵区内には陵廟、寝殿、便殿などの礼制建築が存在し、寝殿と便殿は一般に陵園内或いは陵園付近にある。

7、西漢早中期の諸帝陵には陵邑が置かれ、一般に帝陵の東或いは北側にある。漢元帝時に陵園は廃止される。

8、陪葬墓において、歴史上出現が非常に早く、規模の大きいものは西漢代からである。西漢諸陵の陪葬墓は一般的に２区に分けられ、多くは東司馬道の南北両側に位置し、東西に排をなし、南北に列をなす。その間は壕溝によって分けられる。側室や妃、身分の特殊なものは帝陵の北側と南側に位置する。陪葬墓は級別或いはその他の原因で、墓塚の外形が覆斗形、饅頭形、山形に分けられる。饅頭形が非常に多く、覆斗形が続き、山形は少ない。陪葬墓の周囲には壕溝が巡るものもあり、墓園の平面は多くが正方形を為し、長方形を為すものもある。墓園内には、例えば園邑や祠室など各種の建築遺跡があり、大型陪葬墓の周囲にも数量の異なる　葬墓と陪葬坑がある。

9、大多数の漢陵付近には大型の刑徒墓地が備わっている。陽陵の刑徒墓地は帝陵の西北約1500mに位置し、その間は壕溝で隔絶されている。[24]

帝陵陵園南門の３出闕の発掘は陽陵考古発掘の２つ目の収穫である。闕は中国古代の一種の重要な建築類型で、都城や宮室、陵墓など等級が高く、規格性の高い建築物の大門の外或いは大門に設置される。《漢書霍光伝》“太夫人顯改光時所自造塋制而侈大之，起三出闕。”の記載は西漢以降に一種の闕の使用制度が形成されたことを証明している。即ち“一般官僚可用一對單闕。諸侯，二千石以上用一對二出闕，由一主闕，一子闕構成。”“皇帝則用三出闕，由一主闕與二子闕構成。”[25]ある専門家は夏商時期に闕が出現したと考えているが、目下の所適切な実物と文献の証明は為されていない。《詩経》《左伝》等の文献記載から、西周時期には少なからず証明され、闕は一種の建築形式として既に出現したとされるが、今のところ実物は残っていない。[26]春秋戦国以降、闕の記載は更に木簡や書の上に絶えず現れる。目下、考古発見の闕に関する図案資料は東漢画像石、画像磚、敦煌壁画、唐墓壁画などがあり、実物資料としては四川、山東、河南省等に現存する東漢石闕及び、新たに発掘された唐乾陵乳峰三出闕、宋陵三出闕などである。時代が早く、等級が高く、規模の大きいものは疑いなく漢景帝陽陵帝陵南闕門遺跡ということになる。このため、その発掘は門闕の起源、発展、門闕制度の形成、影響及び、中国古代建築史の研究などに重要な作用を及ぼす。[27]この他、南闕門遺跡からは最古の囲碁盤(磚質)、陶質脊獣と最大の板瓦(残長108、寛さ43.5cm)も出土されている。[28]

数量が多く種類が豊富な陶塑品の大量出土は陽陵考古発掘のもう一つの重大な収穫である。目下、陽陵からは銅器、鉄器、金器、玉器、石器、陶器、漆器、木器、骨器、貝殻、絹織物、麻の各類の器物及び、麦、粟、豆、黍など各類糧食標本など文物約５万点が出土しており、その中でも数量最多で最も特色のあるものは各類の陶俑と陶塑動物を含めた陶塑製品である。

陽陵陶塑は異なる製作工芸から着衣式[29](いわゆる裸体俑)と塑衣式の２大類に分けられる。着衣式の陶俑は帝陵従葬坑、南区従葬坑といくつかの大型陪葬墓の従葬坑内から出土している。塑衣式陶俑の多くは一号建築遺跡と大中型陪葬墓中から出土している。近年来の漢恵帝安陵、武帝茂陵、宣帝杜陵付近及び長安城の制陶作坊などの考古発見を合わせて考えると、当時この種の陶体木腕、彩色の衣を纏った着衣式陶俑は、皇室随葬専用の級別で非常に高い陪葬品であったと確定できる。一般の貴族大臣達は皇帝特賜の状況下においては未だこの類の陶俑を使用することは出来ず、服飾を陶塑した「塑衣式」彩色陶俑しか陪葬出来なかったのである。

陶俑の性別は男性と女性をのぞいて、宦者俑も発見されており[30]、これは中国秦漢考古中最初のものであり、その出土は陶俑の性別類型を補い、中国古代宦官制度史の研究に重要な価値を持っている。

陶俑の形態から現在までに立俑、拱手立俑、執物立俑、跽座俑、俯身俑、舞踏俑、馭馬俑、奏楽俑、行走俑、騎馬俑などが発見されている。また身分からは将軍俑、歩兵俑、騎兵俑、宦者俑、門吏俑、侍女俑、伎楽俑、馭手俑などに分けられる。まとめると、陽陵の陶俑品種は豊富で全てそろっており、数量も非常に多く、地下陵墓中の随葬品として、これらの陶俑は皇家を除いた西漢社会各階層の代表であり、非常に高い研究価値を備えている。

出土した大量の陶俑の分析研究から、着衣式陶俑の製作工芸はだいたい以下の通りである。

1、模制：まず適した陶土を選定し、篩にかけてから、砂利を洗い流すことでより純粋なものとし、乾湿軟硬の適当な陶泥とする。これを準備の出来ている模具の中に流し込む。当時の模具は頭部、体部、腿部、脚部の四つに大きく分けられる。

2、加塑：陶俑の主体部分を成形後更に鼻、耳、陽具などの部品を接着し、鼻、耳、肛門などの部分に孔洞を開ける。模制による陶俑代わり映えしないという弊害を避けるために、工匠達は面部に捏、塑、刻みなどの芸術加工を施し、同じ模制の陶俑の形象をそれぞれの情態にする。最後に俑体の各部分を接合して成形する。

3、焙焼：陶俑の粗製作完成後、陶窯内に入れ焼き、堅い陶質に変化させる。

4、着色：焙焼終了後の陶俑に身体それぞれの部分の状況に応じて彩色する。例えば陶俑の頭髪、眉毛、目、髭などは黒色に塗り、その顔面、体は橙紅色にする。工匠達が彩色時に陶俑の面部に刻み、抹、彩色など更に芸術性を深める加工を行うことで、陶俑は更に生き生きと真に迫るのであり、非常に価値のある作業である。

5、烘焼：陶俑に彩色した色彩を更に緊密にするために、再び炉に入れ焼く。

6、彫刻：陶質の身体の製作と同時に、間接を動かせる木製の腕と手を製作する。

7、組立：製作した木製の腕と手を焼き上がった陶俑の肩部に設けた穿孔部分に装着し、一体の陶俑の基本造形が完成する。次に陶俑の着る装飾、配置や装備などが必要となる。例えば、南、北区従葬坑は軍隊設置に応じており、その中には大量の軍士俑が必要となる。そして、作坊の中には既に出来上がった陶俑が戦服を着、甲冑を纏い、両手には戟を持ち盾を備え、威風凛々とした武士の形象を為し、その後当時の軍隊の隊列に応じて従葬坑に入れられるのである。

付近出土の着衣式陶塑と比較すると建築遺跡や陪葬墓中で出土した塑衣式陶俑製作工芸は比較的簡単で、模制、加塑、焙焼、着色等の段階を経て、彫刻と組立等の工程を減少させている。2000年もの長きに渡る侵食を経て、高級な“衣紈綈”の着衣式陶塑は、木製腕は残るが、彩色の衣服は既に朽ち果て、赤裸々な「醜い」形象で、逆に低級な塑衣式陶俑は昔からの風采を残し、我々に漢代陶塑の人体美の神秘を味わわせてくれるだけでなく、同時に文景盛世の輝きをも楽しませてくれるのである。

これらの彩色着衣式陶俑は2000年にも渡る地下の埋蔵を経て、肩上の木製腕と身体の服装紡織品等の多くは既に朽ちて残っていないが、考古労働者の細かな観察と調査によって、その服装の痕跡をありありと見て取れる。これらの痕跡と塑衣式陶俑の服装を参照にして、陽陵陶俑の服飾状況を理解できたのである。

1，髪型：陽陵陶俑の髪型は櫛で梳かしてきちんと整っており、椎髻、扁髻、円髻など異なる様式がある。

(1)椎髻：全ての髪を頭の後ろに梳かし、そこで縛るものである。この種の垂下式の髻は秦漢時期の婦女の髪型で、ずっと主導の地位を占めており、その形状が木のばちに似ていることから名が付けられた。陽陵の着衣式陶俑中の女俑のほとんどがこの髪型をしているが、男武士俑のいくつかもこの髪型をしている。《漢書・陸賈伝》では“賈至，尉佗，結箕踞見賈。”と記され、服虔の注には“音椎，今兵士椎頭髻也。”とある。当時の兵士中にも椎髻を結っているものが見受けられるのである。

(2)堕馬髻：またの名を堕髻という。梳いているときに真ん中で分け、こめかみを通して頚の後ろでひとまとめにし、髻を引き上げた後背中に垂らす。髻中から引き出した髪を垂らす。この髪型は漢代に始まり、一時期流行したが、東漢以降は結うものが減り、魏晋時代にはほとんど見られなくなった。婦女の髪型の中でも比較的重んじられたものである。陪葬墓園130号墓出土の彩色女俑は全てこの髪型であった。

(3)扁髻：男武士俑、男侍俑及び騎兵俑の一部は頭の後ろで扁髻を結っている。扁髻は形状から大きく2つに分けられ、1つ辮形扁髻、2つ目は未編成辮形扁髻である。辮形扁髻の結い形は2種類あり、1つは全ての髪を頭の後ろに梳き、1本の幅広の辮を作り、さらに辮を頭の後ろで折り、その上方を頭と同じ高さか或いは少し高くし、小さな髻を結い簪を挿して止める。もう1つの結い形は、梳いているときに真ん中で2つに分けこめかみのところでそれぞれ7，8本の小辮を結う。更にその辮を上に上げ頭の後ろで1つにまとめ、簪を挿して頭の上で固定させる。この種の髪型は南区従葬坑出土の騎兵俑に見られる。未編成辮形扁髻は比較的簡単な結い形で、頭髪を全て頭の後ろに梳いて、その髪を頭の後ろで逆に折り返して、頭頂よりやや高いところで髻を結う。髻内に簪を横に挿して固定する。

(4)円髻：南区従葬坑出土の騎兵俑中に頭部が饅頭上に突出したものがおり、その髪型も特殊である。俑頭上には髻の編み目もなく、ただ頭の後ろで円丘形に髻を結っているだけである。結い形はまず髪の毛を梳いて整わせ、それを全て頭の後ろに環形に巻き、余った髪をその環内に入れ、その先を巻いた髪の下に押し込み止める。この種の髪型は古くからの名称がわからず、その円丘形の形状から円髻と仮称しておく。

2，冠式：南区従葬坑出土の多くの陶俑の頭部には、絹織物の痕跡が残っていた。その中の一部分の俑は間違いなく冠を乗せたものにちがいないが、保存状態の関係から多くの俑の冠式は不明である。ここでは、南区従葬坑20号坑出土の2体の俑の頭上の絹織物痕跡から、武士俑の冠式に対しての分析を行いたい。この2体の陶俑の頭部には保存が比較的良好で、俑頭の額部から鬢を経て後頭部に至る、寛さ2cmの朱赤色の痕跡があり、非常に鮮やかである。色彩に残る縦横の編み目紋の観察から、絹織物の痕跡と類似していた。これはおそらく頭髪を束ねる“陌額”であろう。《漢書・周勃伝》に薄太后が“以冒絮提文帝。”の記載がある。応劭は“陌額，絮也。”と注を乗せている。古人は多く長髪を携え、櫛で梳いた後に布帛を用いて額に巻き、“陌額”と称したのである。これは今日のはちまきと同じ様な作用である。俑頭上に乗せた冠の形状は、おそらくちりとりを逆さに伏せたような形で、天辺円形で額部は短く、頭の後ろを長くし、両側にそれぞれ長い耳を垂らす。冠は目の上ではっきりとしており、細長い布帛を用いて作られる。この種の冠は古代の弁に似ており、《釋名・釋首飾》では“弁，如兩手合時也。”と記され、《続漢書・輿服志》では弁を“制如覆杯，前高廣，後卑鋭。”としている。弁の形状はおそらく両手を合わせて伏せた形或いは耳杯を逆さまにしたような形である。ここから、陽陵漢俑頭に乗せられているのは弁であることがわかる。先秦以来、武士は主に弁を乗せていた《周禮・司服》では“凡兵事，韋弁服。”と記されている。咸陽楊家湾の“三千漢俑”も頭に弁を乗せており、陽陵着衣式陶俑の冠式と非常に似ている。

3，衣装：社会風習から、漢代人は袍服を主とし、長衣を重ね着する。この点は陽陵出土の塑衣式陶俑上の表現から十分明らかである。この類の陶俑の着ている塑服装の様子ははっきりしており、衣装の着方も清楚で、以下の特徴があげられる。

1、衣装は相重なり、腰のところで縫い合わされる。

2、短領で、領を方折する様式である。

3、衣襟は長いものを斜角にし、前で巻き後ろに回し、中の衣が見えないようにする。これらは長衣の基本的な特徴である。長衣はまたの名を“深衣”と言い、春秋時代に出現し、戦国、西漢で盛んとなる。男女や尊卑を問わず着られ、その体に深く纏う様子から名付けられた。陽陵の塑衣式陶俑は性別、身分などを問わず、ほとんど深衣を着ており、当時の深衣制の盛んな様を更に説明している。

着衣式陶俑の衣服は既に朽ち、その様式は判断しがたい。南区従葬坑出土の着衣式陶俑から言うと、その身分はほとんどが武士で、行軍作戦が必要であり、漢代の深衣、袍服は普通裾口が開かず袖が大きいため、走行には不便であったため、深衣或いは袍服を着ていることはあまり現実的ではない。秦始皇陵と楊家湾漢墓で出土した塑衣式武士俑中、多くの陶俑はほとんどが長さが膝までしかない長襦を着ていた。長襦と袍服の区別は長さの違いで、深衣と袍服は足までの長さで、長襦の長さは膝までである。南区従葬坑の調査中に発見した裸俑の衣物痕跡から、陽陵の着衣式武士俑の上衣も膝付近までしかなく、長襦を着ていたに違いない。この衣服は比較的短く、袖口は細く、動くのに非常に便利なため、着衣式武士俑が長襦を着ていたことは当時の実際状況に合っている。

大部分の武士俑の腿の部分は、朱赤色の織物を着ており、斜めに巻かれている痕跡から明らかに“行藤”である。漢軍の行藤は大きな布帛を用い、角を繋いで帯にし、まず帯の上方で横に縛り、更に斜めに巻いて下を“Z”形にし、腿の後ろで堅く結ぶ。《釋名》では“幅，所以自偪束，今謂行，言以裹腿。”と記載されている。この種の行藤は、近代軍隊中における戦士の脚絆である。楊家湾漢墓の騎兵と歩兵俑群及び秦俑坑内武士俑の臑部に巻かれた形と行藤が似ており、秦漢時代にこの種の服飾が比較的流行したことの証明となる。

4，甲冑：南区従葬坑からはまた甲冑を纏った武士俑が出土し、甲片は皮製で、出土時には朽ちていたが、紅色と黒色の痕跡が残っていた。痕跡の調査から、鎧甲の甲片は正方形で、辺長2cm、毎片の中部には上下左右に甲片を繋ぐ２つの小孔がある。前甲上部甲片は中線から外側に甲片を重ね、上から下に重ねて６層を形成し、紐で結ばれている。前甲下部は上から下に喇叭上に広がり、下から上に重ねて４層を形成し、左から右に重ねている。後甲は中線両側の甲片の配列方法が前甲と逆になる。腕部には２層の甲片を纏っている。[31]この類の甲はその甲片形が簡札に似ていることから、文献中では札甲と称される。漢代の鎧を纏った武士俑の形成は楊家湾漢墓陪葬坑で出土した陶俑が最も具体的な例である。ここの俑の多くは札甲を纏い、簡単な類型では胸・背を護る程度で、複雑なものはそれに腕部と腰部下に垂れる腹甲が付け加わる。[32]楊家湾漢墓陪葬坑の時代と性質は陽陵南区従葬坑のものと大体同じであり、調査時に発見した痕跡から見て、陽陵の鎧を纏った武士俑の甲式もそれと同類と思われる。

5，鞋履：秦漢時期の靴履は主に履、屦、舄、鞋、靴等があるが、正規の場合には漢代人は履を穿いていた。陽陵塑衣式陶俑が穿いているのも基本的には履である。着衣式陶俑の足部からは鞋履の痕跡は見つかっていないが、その他の部位の着衣状況から判断して、足部の履き物を省略することはあり得ない。また性質の似ている楊家湾漢墓の陪葬坑から出土した陶俑の脚部では鞋履を穿いており、その形式は草履式の“芒鞋”、先が尖り上を向く“　履”、浅幫円口鞋、高腰綉花靴の４種に分けられる。[33]陽陵の着衣式陶俑の鞋履形式は上述の楊家湾陶俑と基本的に相似しており、一般武士俑の多くは草履、騎兵俑は浅幫円口鞋、それ以外の２種類は比較的少ない。

製作技術と造形の風格から見て、陽陵の陶俑は２つの異なる文化と埋葬制度の影響を受けた産物と考えられる。陽陵で大量に随葬された陶俑及び塑衣式陶俑の工芸造形と秦始皇帝兵馬俑坑出土の陶俑は基本的に一致しており、秦の帝陵埋葬制度の影響を受けたことは疑いない。しかし、多くの塑衣式陶俑が纏う「深衣」は楚文化の明らかな特徴の１つである。

着衣式陶俑に腕をはめ込み、外側に絹織物の衣服を着る作り方は明らかに秦俑とは異なり、この種の製法は目下楚俑でしか認められない。湖北江陵雨花台、湖南長沙等の楚墓においてこの類の着衣式木俑が多く出土している。この種の習俗は後に原楚国の領地内の西漢墓に踏襲されるのである。中国建国後に発掘した長沙馬王堆では冠を被った着衣式男俑が２体、着衣仆女俑が10体、着衣歌舞俑が８体出土しており、俑の体は木製で体は彫刻で輪郭を表し、両腕はなく、体には羅綺でできた衣服を着ていた。[34]これらから、陽陵出土の裸体着衣式陶俑は楚の影響下における産物であると確定できる。

陽陵の陶塑動物における主なものは馬、牛、羊、犬、鶏などで、これらの動物俑の製作工芸も非常に凝っており、塑衣式陶俑の模制、加塑、焙焼、着色などの加工工程を経たのち、着衣式陶俑制作中における彫刻、組装等の工芸(牛、羊、馬などの角や尾を木製で作り組み立てる)をも採用している。

陽陵の陶塑動物の種類は多く、非常に生き生きとしており、生活情緒に富んでいる。陶牛の体はがっしりとして大きく、4腿は強健で首は短く、両耳は斜めに伸び、両目は外側に膨らみ、屈強で力のある牛の気質を表現している。陶綿羊は体が丸く、両足が細長く、両耳は斜めに垂れ、口はやや広がり,臀部は大きく尻尾は垂れ下がっている。陶山羊は体に丸みを帯び、足は柱のように真っ直ぐで耳は立ち、髭が垂れ下がり、小さな尾は上に跳ね、おっとりした表情で、おとなしく、かわいらしさを現している。陶豚は体は大きく太っており、４足は短く、お腹が垂れ、腹下には２つの乳頭があり、首は短く、口は長く耳は大きく、無邪気でかわいらしい。陶犬は狼犬と家犬に分けられ、狼犬は両耳が斜めに立ち、両目は前方を凝視し、口は細長く、両頬は膨らみ、首が短く、体はがっしりとしており、４足には力があり、尾は下に垂れる。家犬は両耳が直立し、両目がやや膨らみ、口はやや短く、体には膨らみがあり４足はがっしりし、尾は上に巻く。２種類の犬の造形は、真に迫り、人々に凛然として犯しがたい態度を与える。陶鶏は雄雌２種に別れ、体全体に彩色され、その色彩は非常に鮮やかである。雄鶏h首を擡げ、尾を上に跳ねらせ、嘴は長く、目は小さく、朱赤色の鶏冠を持ち、黒・紅・黄の３色の羽毛を持つ。母鶏は体がやや小さく尾が短く、頭部には鶏冠が無く、非常に真に迫っている。陶塑動物の数量は多く、造形美においても前代未聞のものである。[35]

各類の陶俑と動物彫刻から成る陽陵陶塑は政治・経済・軍事・文化などを含めた西漢社会における全方位的な情報を持っており、我々の漢代歴史の理解、把握、研究に対して重要な史料価値を備え、同時に非常に高い芸術価値をも持っている。目下の全体における初歩的研究から、陽陵陶塑は一方では秦俑の「写実的芸術風格」、「人体的造形特色」、「神韻の重視」、「爛熟した技法」、「彩色と塑の結合した技法」そして、「制作工芸の多様化」等の芸術伝統を継承し[36]同時に基礎上の前代からの型に填った模式を棄て、楚文化の造形芸術の精華を汲み、「写意的な芸術表現手法」、「彩色、彫刻、塑、着の結合技法」、「形態の重視」そして、「浪漫主義の手法」等の芸術特徴を創造し、精緻で生き生きとしたものにし、生活情緒に富んだ新しい息吹を与え、我が国古代彫塑芸術を新たな段階に発展させたのである。

(1)《史記・孝景本紀》

(2)《漢書・景帝紀》

(3)《漢書・景帝紀》

(4)《漢書・外戚傳》

(5)焦南峰:《漢代京城、帝陵的考古發掘和研究》、待刊稿。

(6)秦中行:《漢陽陵附近鉗徒墓的發現》,《考古》,1976年12期。

(7)王丕忠、張子波、孫德潤:《漢景帝陽陵調查簡報》,《考古與文物》,1980年第一期。

(8)劉慶柱、李毓芳:《西漢諸陵調查與研究》,《文物資料叢刊》,第六輯,1982年。劉慶柱、李毓芳:《西漢十一陵》,陝西人民出版社1987年7月。

(9)陝西省考古研究所漢陵考古隊:《漢景帝陽陵南區從葬坑第一號簡報》,《文物》,1992年第四期。陝西省考古研究所漢陵考古隊:《漢景帝陽陵南區從葬坑第二號簡報》,《文物》,1994年第四期。陝西省考古研究所漢陵考古隊:《中國漢陽陵彩俑》陝西旅游出版社,1992年。

(10)焦南峰、王保平、馬永嬴、李崗等:《漢景帝陽陵發現陪葬墓園》,《中國文物報》,1999年11月14日。《漢陽陵園内發現大批從葬坑出土大量珍貴文物》,《中國文物報》,1999年11月28日。

(11)陝西省考古研究所陽陵考古隊:《漢景帝陽陵考古新發現》,《文博》, 1999年第6期。

(12)焦南峰、王保平、馬永嬴、李崗:《漢陽陵園内發現大批從葬坑出土大量珍貴文物》,《中國文物報》, 1999年11月28日。

(13)發掘尚未結束, 資料存陽陵考古隊。

(14)同上

(15)同上

(16)焦南峰、王保平、馬永嬴、李崗:《漢陽陵園内發現大批從葬坑出土大量珍貴文物》,《中國文物報》, 1999年11月28日。

(17)陝西省考古研究所陽陵考古隊:《漢景帝陽陵考古新發現》,《文博》, 1999年第六期。

(18)陝西省考古研究所漢陵考古隊:《中國漢陽陵彩俑》陝西旅游出版社, 1992年。

(19)董鴻聞等:《陽陵羅經石的實測和研究》,《測繪通報》, 1995年6期。

(20)焦南峰:《漢代京城、帝陵的考古發掘和研究》、待刊稿。

(21)秦中行:《漢陽陵附近鉗徒墓的發現》,《考古》, 1976年12期。

(22)《漢書·高惠高后文功臣表》。

(23)焦南峰、王保平、馬永嬴、李崗:《漢景帝陽陵發現陪葬墓園》,《中國文物報》, 1999年11月14日。

(24)焦南峰、馬永嬴:《西漢帝陵無昭穆制度論》,《文博》, 1999年5期。

(25)趙化成:《從"商周公墓制"到秦漢"獨立陵園制"的歷史軌迹》,《古代文明研究通訊(摘要)》, 2000年六期。

(26)焦南峰:《漢代京城、帝陵的考古發掘和研究》, 待刊稿。

(27)孫機:《漢代物質文化資料圖説·闕, 闕門》,《文物出版社》, 1991年。

(28)重慶市文化局、重慶市博物館:《四川漢代石闕》, 文物出版社, 1992年。

(29)焦南峰:《漢家陵闕》,《中國文物報》, 1999年11月30日。

(30)李崗:《漢陽陵園棋棋局》,《中國文物報》, 1999年12月5日。

(31)王學理:《着衣式木臂陶俑的時代意義》,《文博》, 1997年第六期。

(32)資料存陽陵考古隊。

(33)陝西省考古研究所漢陵考古隊:《漢景帝陽陵南區從葬坑第二號簡報》,《文物》, 1994年第四期。

(34)楊秉禮、史宇闊等:《西漢三千彩繪兵馬俑》, 陝西人民美術出版社, 1996年。

(35)楊秉禮、史宇闊等:《西漢三千彩繪兵馬俑》, 陝西人民美術出版社, 1996年。

(36)湖南省博物館、中國社會科學院考古研究所:《長沙馬王堆一號漢墓》, 文物出版社, 1973年。

(37)王保平:《精美的漢代動物雕塑》,《中國文物報》, 1999年11月30日。

(38)袁仲一:《秦始皇陵兵馬俑研究》, 文物出版社, 1990年。

一、夕阳下的汉阳陵
Han Yangling Mausoleum under the evening sun

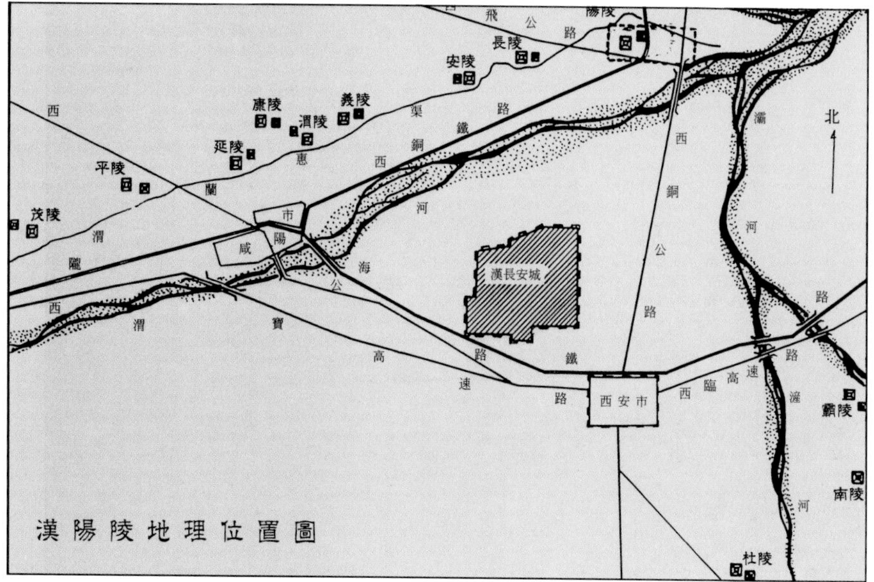

二、汉阳陵地理位置图
The geographic location of Yangling

三、汉阳陵陵区彩红外影像图 ►
An infrared color photo of Yangling

西汉景帝阳陵彩红外影像图
图例
1998
陕西省文物管理局
0 100 200 300

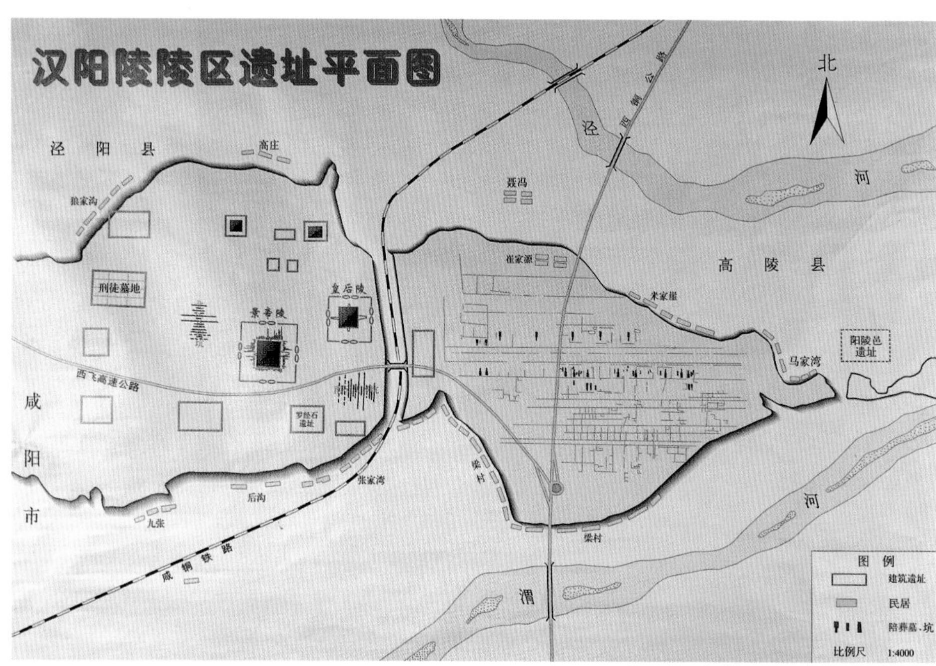

五、汉阳陵陵区平面图
Plan map of Han Yangling

四、汉阳陵东侧的“泾渭之会”
A map showing the Jing River joining the Wei River in the east of Yangling

五、咸阳原上的汉阳陵

七、咸阳原上的汉阳陵
Han Yangling on the Xianyang plain

六、汉阳陵外景
A full view of the Emperor's and Empress's tombs

八、“泾置阳陵”瓦当拓片
面径：15.3厘米。
A rubbing from an earthenware eaves tile which read "Jingzhi Yangling" the Jing River flows by Yangling

九、“阳陵□”戳印瓦片►
长14、宽3.5厘米六号建筑遗址出土
A rubbing from the inscriptions of an eaves tile bearing the words "Yangling"

一〇、汉景帝陵外景
The Mausoleum of the Emperor Jingdi

一一、王皇后陵外景
The Mausoleum of the Empress

漢陽陵帝陵陵園平面圖

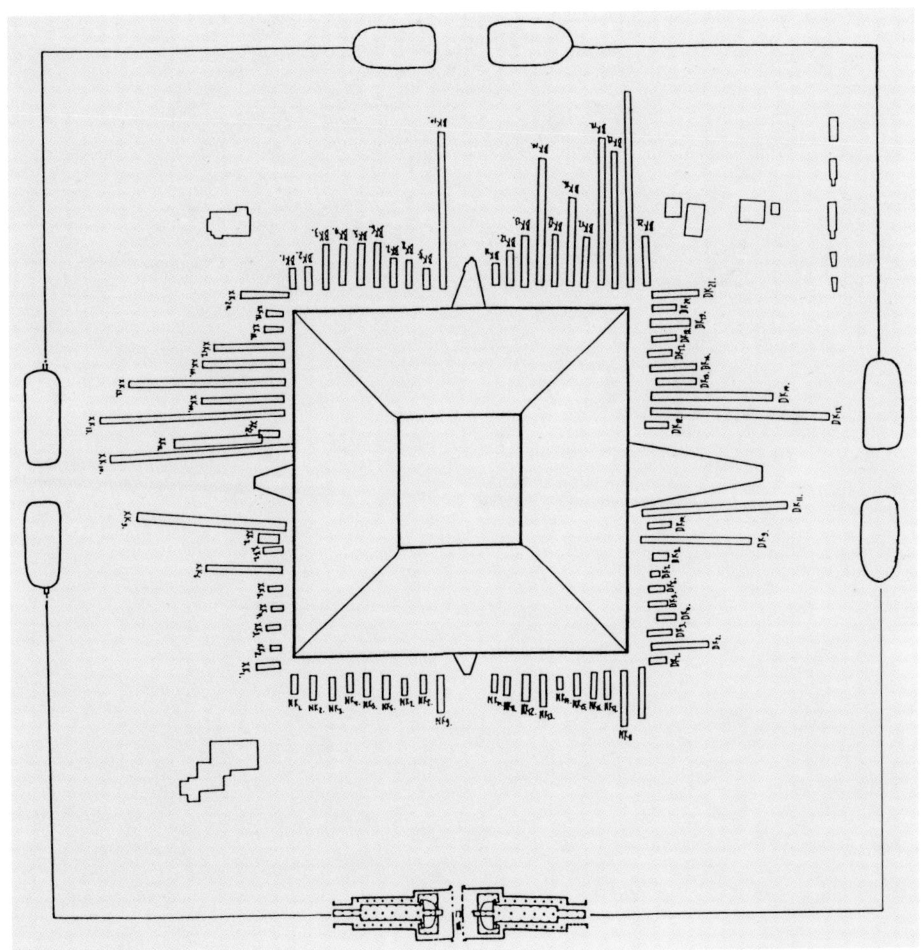

一二、汉阳陵帝陵陵园平面图
Plan map of the entire burial ground

一三、帝陵东侧从葬坑（鸟瞰）
The pits containing burial objects on the east of the Emperor's tomb

一四、帝陵东侧 13 号从葬坑的棚木遗迹
Traces of the wooden planks of No.13 burial pit on the east of the Emperor's tomb

一五、考古工作者正在清理帝陵东侧 11 号从葬坑中的文物
Archaeologists excavating artifacts in No.11 burial pit on the eastern side of the Emperor's tomb

一六、帝陵东侧 11 号从葬坑清理出土的木马和陶骑兵俑
Wooden horses and pottery figures of mounted soldiers unearthed from No.11 burial pit

一七、帝陵东侧 11 号从葬坑清理出土的木车轮遗迹
Traces of wooden wheels unearthed from No.11 burial pit

一八、帝陵东侧 11 号从葬坑出土的骑兵俑
Pottery figures of mounted soldiers
unearthed from No.11 burial pit

一九、彩绘陶塑动物群（自西向东拍摄）
Painted pottery figures of animals
Unearthed from No.13 burial pit on
the eastern side of the Emperor's
tomb (picture taken from west to east)

二〇、彩绘陶塑动物群

帝陵东侧 13 号从葬坑出土

Painted pottery figures of animals

Unearthed from No.13 burial pit on the eastern side of the Emperor's tomb

二一、彩绘陶塑绵羊群

帝陵东侧 13 号从葬坑出土

Painted pottery figures of sheep

Unearthed from No.13 burial pit on the eastern side of the Emperor's tomb

二二、彩绘陶塑狗

帝陵东侧 13 号从葬坑出土

Painted pottery figures of dogs

Unearthed from No.13 burial pit on the east of the Emperor's tomb

二三、帝陵东侧 13 号从葬坑出土的木车马遗迹

Traces of the wooden chariot and horses in No.13 burial pit on the east of the Emperor's tomb

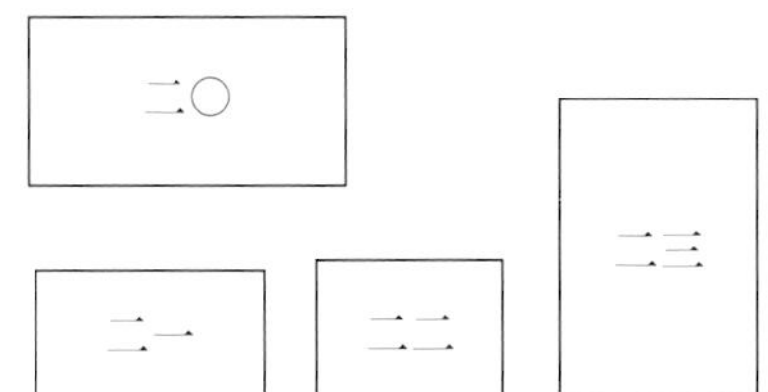

◀ 二四、帝陵陵园西北隅的排水系统
The sewer system in the northwestern corner of the burial ground

二五、帝陵与南阙门遗址
The Emperor's Mausoleum and the South Gate

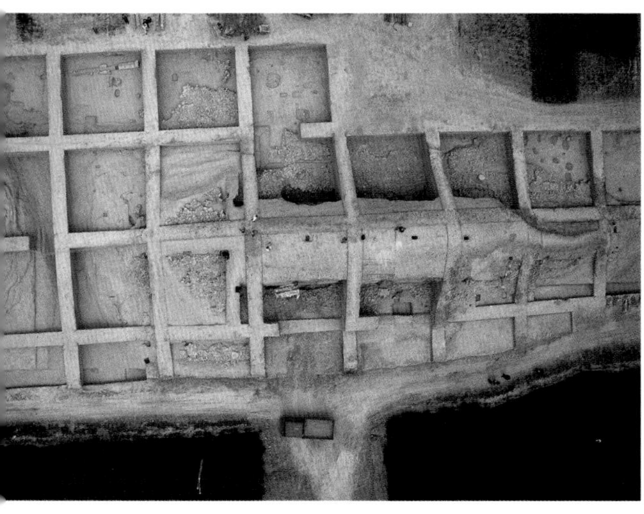

二六、正在发掘中的帝陵南阙门遗址
Ruins of the south gate under excavation work

二七、发掘中的帝陵南阙门遗址中部（由北向南）
Excavation work carried out at the middle part of the South Gate ruins (from north to south)

二八、帝陵南阙门遗址主阙台上清理出的柱洞
Post holes unearthed from the main platform of the South Gate ruins

二九、帝陵南阙门遗址的夯土阙台和瓦片堆积
Rammed earth and tile fragments from the main platform of the South Gate ruins

三〇、帝陵南阙门遗址清理出的卵石散水和瓦片堆积 ▶
Pebble stones and tile fragments unearthed from the South Gate

三一、帝陵南阙门的夯土台阶
Rammed steps of the South Gate

三二、发掘后的帝陵南阙门遗址
A bird eye view of the South Gate of the Mausoleum

羅經石遺址平面圖

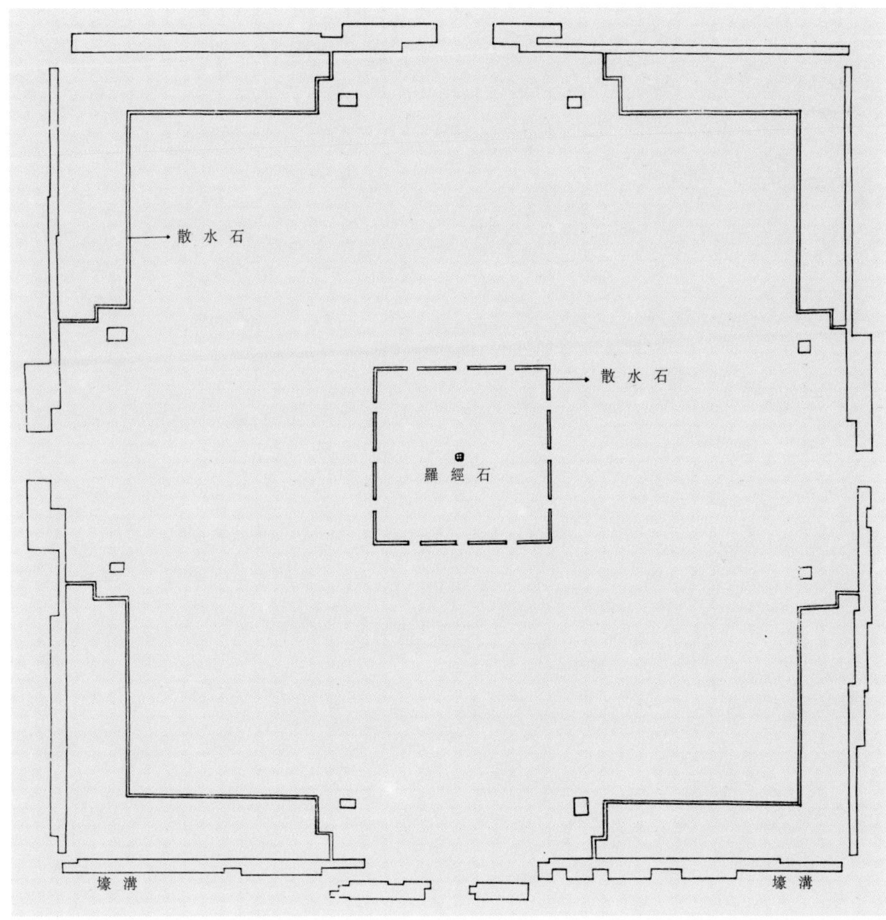

三三、"罗经石"遗址平面图
Plan map of the ruins of the pelorus

三四、"罗经石"与帝、后二陵
The position of the pelorus with the Emperor's and Empress's tombs

三五、"罗经石"

位于景帝陵东南约450米，
直径1.4米，
中心刻有"十"字凹槽，
标示正方向。

"The pelorus"

The pelorus is set at about 450m to the southeast of the Mausoleum with a diameter of 1.4m and a cross carved in the face pointing to the square east, south, west, and north.

三六、“罗经石” 遗址外回廊清理出的瓦片和散水

Tile fragments and pebble stones unearthed from the ruins of the pelorus

三七、南区 20 号从葬坑考古发掘现场
A picture showing the excavation work of No.20 burial pit in the southern rea of the Mausoleum

三八、南区 20 号从葬坑出土着衣式彩绘陶俑群
Painted figures wearing clothes unearthed from No.20 burial pit in the southern area of the Mausoleum

三九、南区 20 号从葬坑清理出土的铠甲武士俑
Pottery figures of the armored warriors unearthed from No.20 burial pit

四〇、保留有木质臂膊及铠甲遗迹的武士陶俑
Pottery figures of warriors with traces of wooden arms and armor-plates

四一、重见天日的勇士们
南区 10 号从葬坑出土
Once more seeing the light of day
Pottery warriors unearthed from No.10 burial pit in the southern area of the Mausoleum

四二、屡经劫难、英气犹存
南区 10 号从葬坑出土
Pottery warriors-enduring many times of raiding without losing his army might
Unearthed from N0.10 burial pit in the southern area

四三、南区 21 号从葬坑出土的陶塑动物
Pottery figures of animals unearthed from No.21 burial pit in the southern area

四四、南区 20 号从葬坑清理出土的彩绘陶鸡
A painted pottery cock unearthed from No.20 burial pit in the southern area

四五、南区 20 号从葬坑清理出土的陶炉台
An earthenware cooking stove unearthed from No.20 burial pit in the southern area

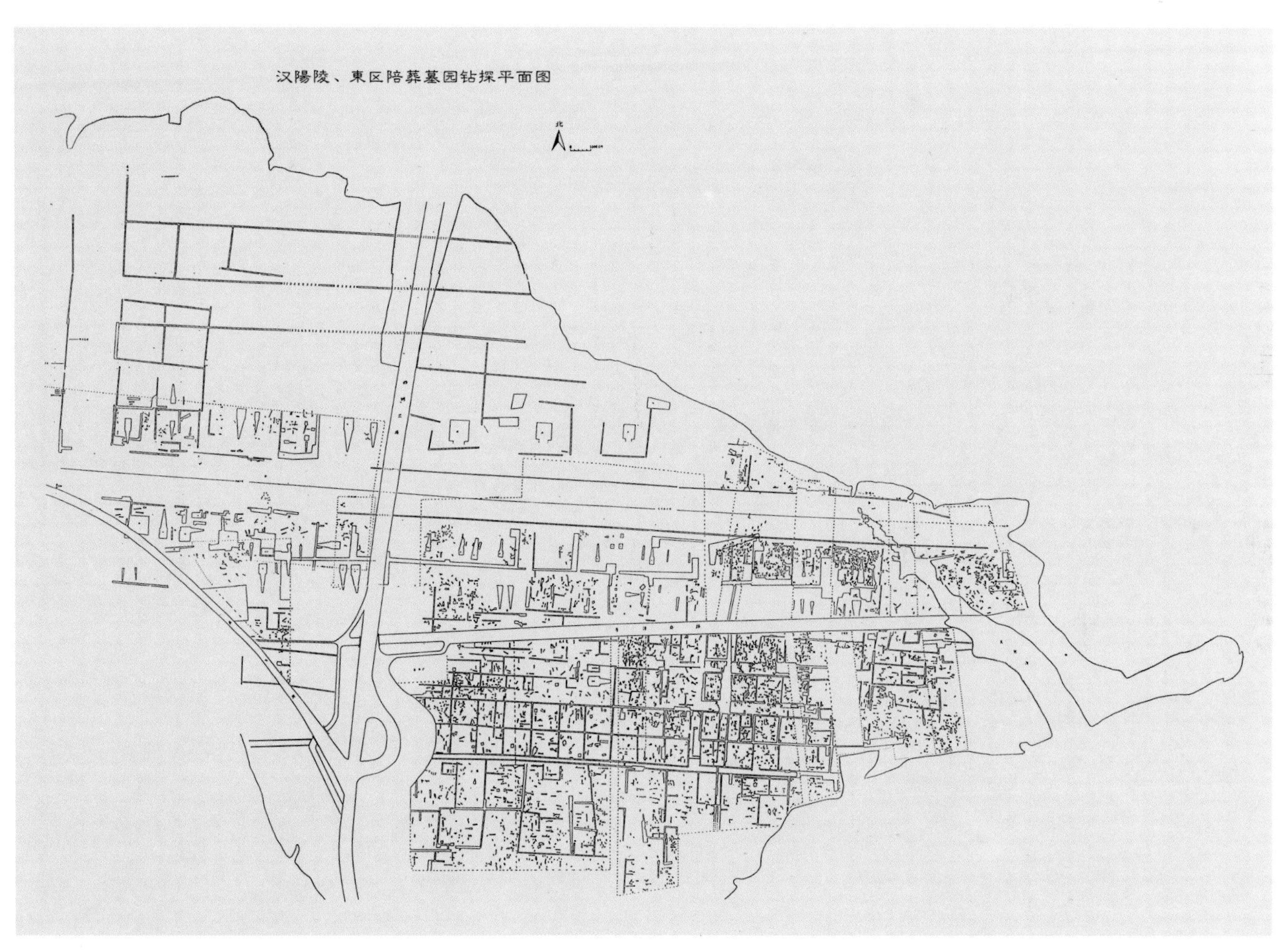

四六、汉阳陵陪葬墓园平面图

Plan map of the accom panying burial pits in Yangling

四七、阳陵陪葬墓外景
Pictures showing the accompanying burial ground

陪葬墓“升子冢”
A sheng-shaped burial tomb

陪葬墓“斗冢”
A dou-shaped burial tomb

陪葬墓“五女冢之一”
Number one of the Five-lady burial tomb

陪葬墓“五女冢之二”
Number two of the Five-lady burial tomb

四八、带有多层台阶的大型陪葬墓发掘现场
全长47米、深16.9米。
Excavation work in a grand burial tomb with many staircases
47m long and 16.9m deep

四九、刚出土的彩绘陶鼎

陪葬墓园出土

A painted pottery ding (cooking vessel) just unearthed

Unearthed from the accompanying burial ground

五〇、刚清理出的铜、骨质的车马器

陪葬墓园出土

Bronze and bone parts of chariots just unearthed

Unearthed from the accompanying burial ground

五一、小型陪葬墓及随葬器物

陪葬墓园出土

A small size accompanying burial pit with some burial objects

Unearthed from the accompanying burial ground

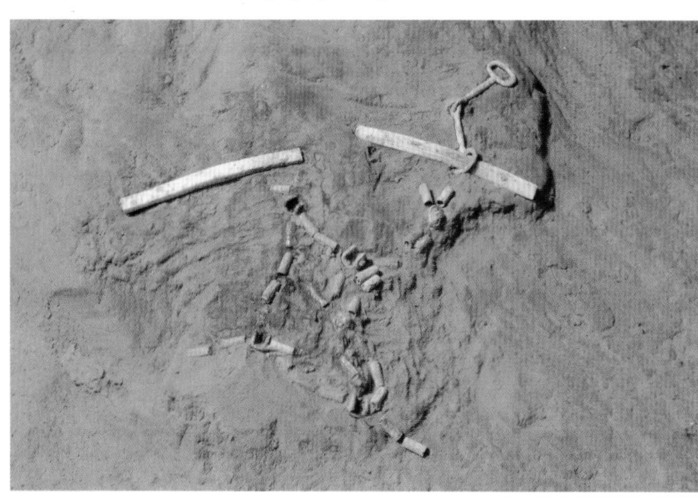

五二、彩绘着衣式骑马陶俑（上半身）

帝陵东侧 11 号从葬坑出土

Painted pottery figures of mounted warriors wearing clothes (the upper body)

Unearthed from No.11 burial pit on the eastern side of the Emperor's tomb

五三、行进中的铠甲武士俑
身高 55 厘米。
南区 20 号从葬坑出土
Pottery figures of the armored warriors who are walking
55cm tall
Unearthed from No.20 burial pit in the southern area

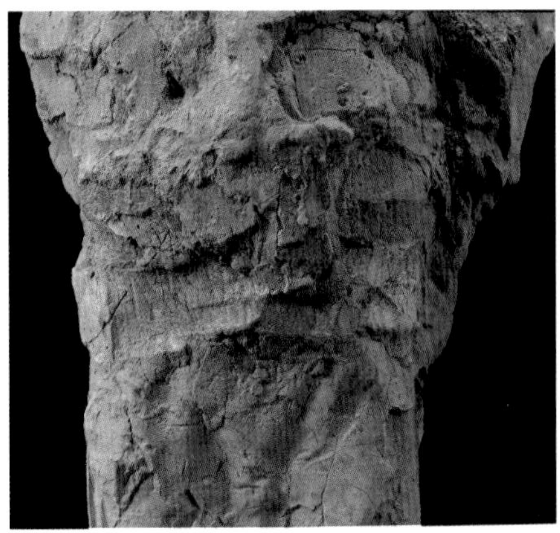

五五、陶俑身上的铠甲及腰带遗迹

南区 20 号从葬坑出土

Traces of the armor-plate and the belt on the pottery warriors

Unearthed from No.20 burial pit in the southern area

五四、上着铠甲下穿战袍的武士俑

身高 57.6 厘米。

南区 20 号从葬坑出土

A pottery warrior wearing a suit of armor and a war robe

57.6cm tall

Unearthed from No.20 burial pit in the southern area

五六、惟妙惟肖的着衣式陶俑

身高 56 —— 59 厘米。

南区从葬坑出土

Pottery figures that look remarkably true to life

56-59cm tall

Unearthed from the burial pits in the southern area of the Mausoleum

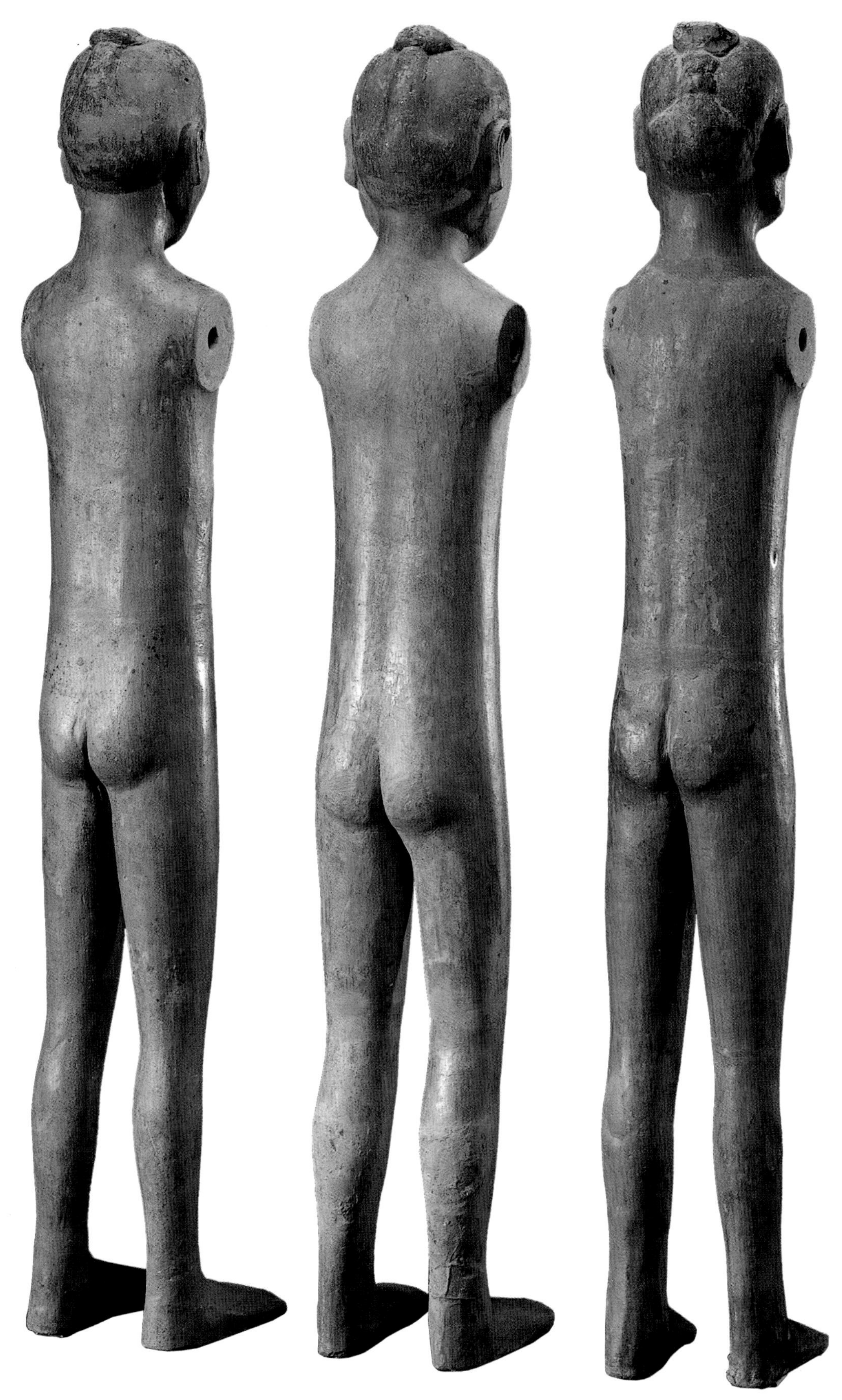

五七、着衣式陶俑背部
南区从葬坑出土
Backs of pottery figures
Unearthed from the burial pits in the southern area of the Mausoleum

五八、着衣式陶俑头部残留的“陌额”和“武弁”遗迹
南区 20 号从葬坑出土
Traces of a headband and a warrior's hat on the pottery heads
Unearthed from No.20 burial pit in the southern area

五九、陶俑鬓侧的武弁遗迹

南区 20 号从葬坑出土

Traces of the warrior's hat on the temple of a pottery figure

Unearthed from No.20 burial pit in the southern area

六〇、神态各异的陶俑
——老成持重
南区从葬坑出土
Pottery figures with various expressions-experienced and prudent
Unearthed in the southern area of the burial pits

六一、神态各异的陶俑——喜上眉梢
南区从葬坑出土
Pottery figures with various expressi-ons-be radiant with joy
Unearthed in the southern area of the burial pits

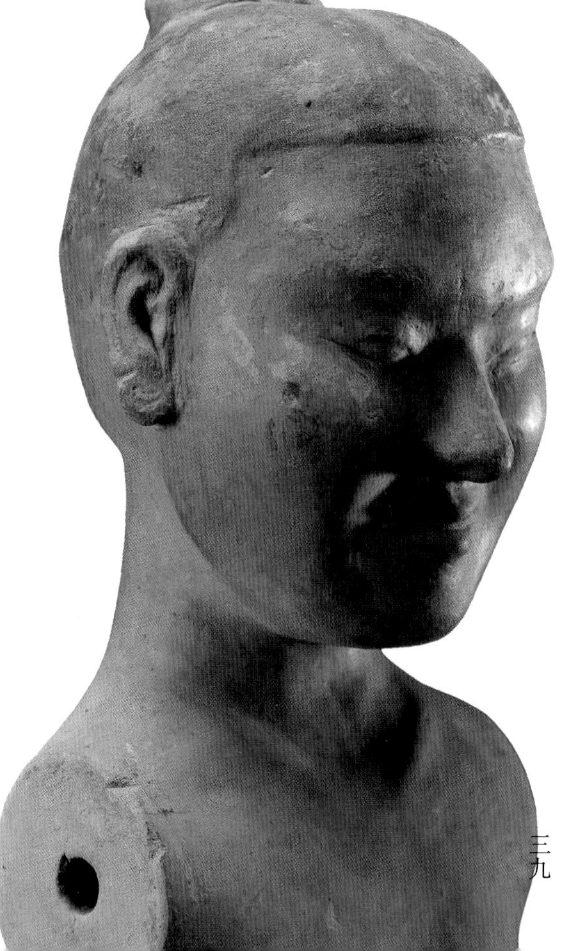

六二、神态各异的陶俑——若有所思
南区从葬坑出土
Pottery figures with various expressions-seem lost in thought
Unearthed in the southern area of the burial pits

六三、神态各异的陶俑——愁眉苦脸

南区从葬坑出土

Pottery figures with various expressions-wear a worried look

Unearthed in the southern area of the burial pits

六四、神态各异的陶俑——心事重重
南区从葬坑出土
Pottery figures with various expressions-be laden with anxiety
Unearthed in the southern area of the burial pits

六五、神态各异的陶俑——率真稚气
南区从葬坑出土
Pottery figures with various expressions-sincere and innocent
Unearthed in the southern area of the burial pits

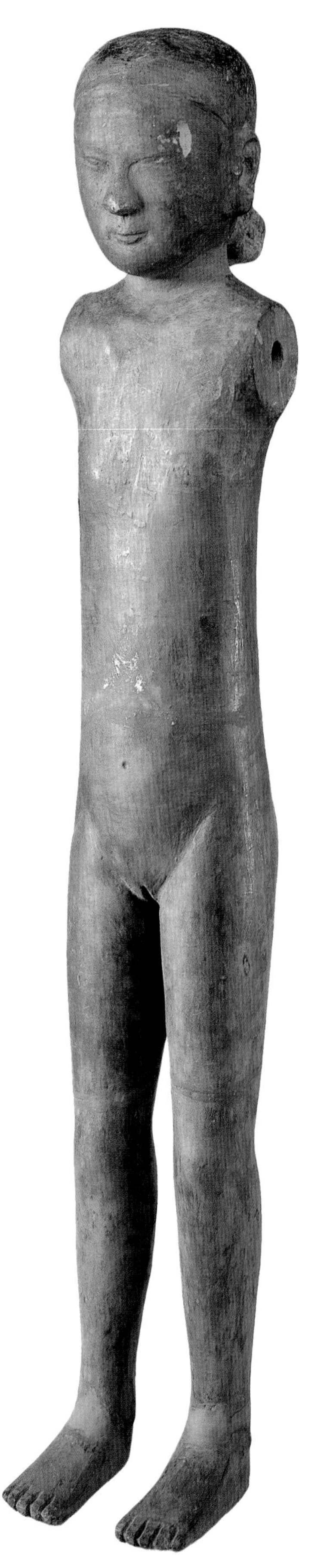

六六 、着衣式彩绘陶女俑
身高53厘米。
陪葬墓园出土
A painted female pottery figure wearing clothes
53cm tall
Unearthed from the accompanying burial ground

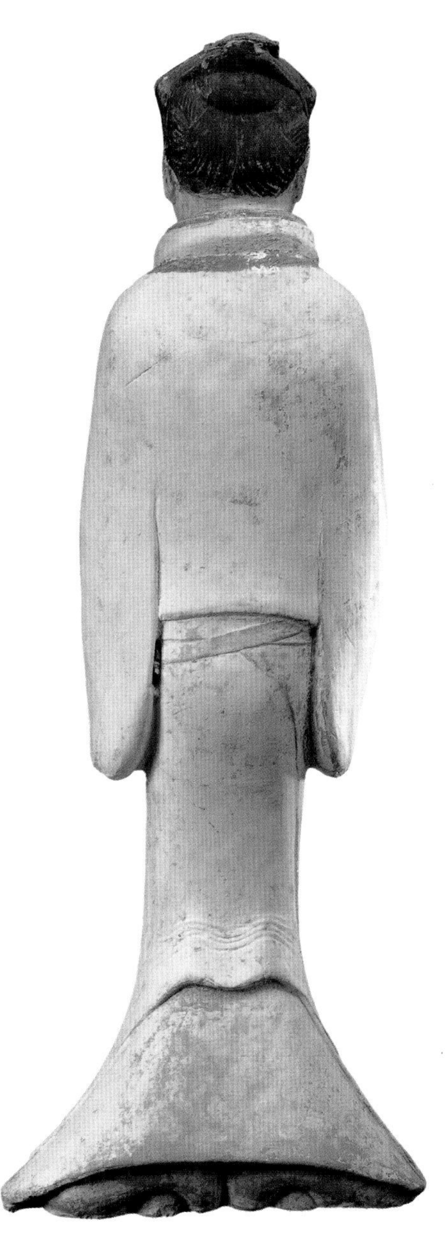

六七、塑衣式彩绘男侍俑

身高 63 厘米。

陪葬墓园出土

Painted pottery figures of male servants with molded clothes

63cm tall

Unearthed from the accompanying burial ground

六八、塑衣式彩绘男侍俑

身高63厘米。

陪葬墓园出土

A painted pottery figure of a male servant with molded clothes

63cm tall

Unearthed from the accompanying burial ground

六九、塑衣式彩绘侍女俑

身高63厘米。

陪葬墓园出土

Painted pottery maids with molded clothes

63cm tall

Unearthed from the accompanying burial ground

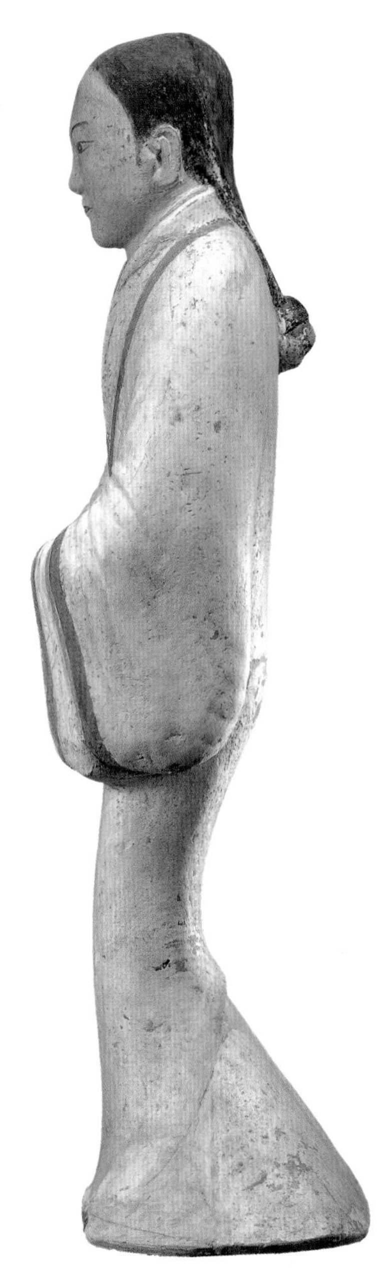

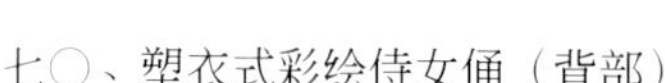

七〇、塑衣式彩绘侍女俑（背部）

身高 63 厘米。

陪葬墓园出土

A painted pottery maid with molded clothes (seen from the back)

63cm tall

Unearthed from the accompanying burial ground

七一、塑衣式彩绘跽坐侍女俑

高 41 厘米。

陪葬墓园出土

A painted pottery maid in the kneeling position

41cm tall

Unearthed from the accompanying burial ground

七二、塑衣式彩绘跽坐侍女俑

高33.5厘米。

陪葬墓园出土

A painted pottery maid in the kneeling position

33.5cm tall

Unearthed from the accompanying burial ground

七三、塑衣式跽坐拱手俑
高33厘米。
陪葬墓园出土
A kneeling pottery maid in the gesture of salutation
33cm tall
Unearthed from the accompanying burial ground

七四、塑衣式跽坐拱手俑（侧面）
高 33 厘米。
陪葬墓园出土
A kneeling pottery maid in the gesture of salutation
33cm tall
Unearthed from the accompanying burial ground

七五、彩绘陶牛

身长71厘米，

高39厘米。

陪葬墓园出土

A painted pottery ox

Lengh:71cm, height:39cm

Unearthed from the accompanying burial ground

七六、彩绘陶绵羊 A
身长 43 厘米，
高 37 厘米。
帝陵东侧从葬坑出土
A painted pottery sheep A
Length:43cm,
height:37cm
Unearthed from the accompanying pits of the Emperor's tomb

七七、彩绘陶绵羊 B
身长 43 厘米，
高 37 厘米。
帝陵东侧从葬坑出土
A painted pottery sheep B
Length:43cm,
height:37cm
Unearthed from the accompanying pits of the Emperor's tomb

七八、彩绘陶山羊 A

身长 44 厘米，

高 32 厘米。

帝陵东侧从葬坑出土

A painted pottery goat A

Length: 40cm，

height:32cm

Unearthed from the accompanying pits of the Emperor's tomb

七九、彩绘陶山羊 B

身长 40 厘米，

高 32 厘米。

帝陵东侧从葬坑出土

A painted pottery sheep B

Length: 40cm,

height:32cm

Unearthed from the accompanying pits of the Emperor's tomb

八〇、彩绘陶公猪
身长44厘米，
高22.5厘米。
帝陵东侧从葬坑出土
A painted pottery boar
Length: 44cm, height: 22.5cm
Unearthed from the accompanying pits of the Emperor's tomb

八一、彩绘陶母猪 A

身长 41 厘米，
高 22.5 厘米。
帝陵东侧从葬坑出土

A painted pottery pig A

Length: 41cm,
height:22.5cm
Unearthed from the accompanying pits of the Emperor's tomb

八二、彩绘陶母猪 B
身长 41 厘米，
高 23 厘米。
帝陵东侧从葬坑出土
A painted pottery pig B
Length: 41cm,
height:23cm
Unearthed from the accompanying pits of the Emperor's tomb

八三、彩绘陶犬

身长31厘米，
高20.5厘米。
帝陵东侧从葬坑出土

A painted pottery dog

Length:31cm,
height:20.5cm
Unearthed from the accompanying pits of the Emperor's tomb

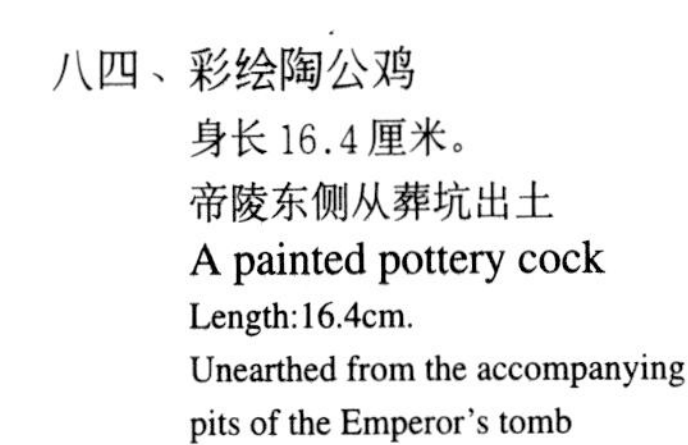

八四、彩绘陶公鸡

身长16.4厘米。

帝陵东侧从葬坑出土

A painted pottery cock

Length:16.4cm.

Unearthed from the accompanying pits of the Emperor's tomb

八五、彩绘陶鸡

身长 16.3、15 厘米，

高 14.8 、11 厘米。

帝陵东侧从葬坑出土

Painted pottery chickens

Length:16.3cm, 15cm,

height: 14.8cm, 11cm

Unearthed from the accompanying pits of the Emperor's tomb

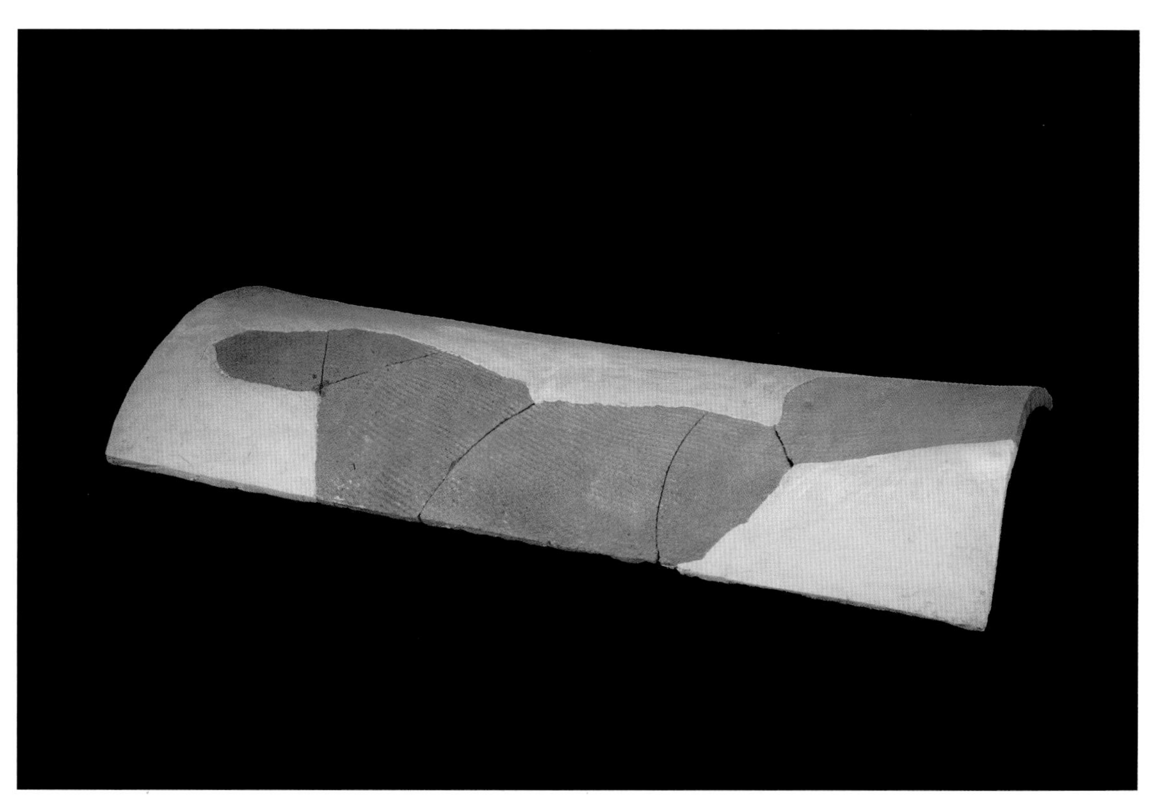

八六、板瓦
残长 112 厘米。
帝陵南阙门遗址出土
Pan tiles
Length (damaged): 112cm
Unearthed at the ruins of the South Gate

八七、筒瓦
长50.6厘米，
宽 16.2 厘米。
帝陵南阙门遗址出土
Semi tube-shaped tile
Length: 50.6cm,
width: 16.2cm
Unearthed at the ruins of the South Gate

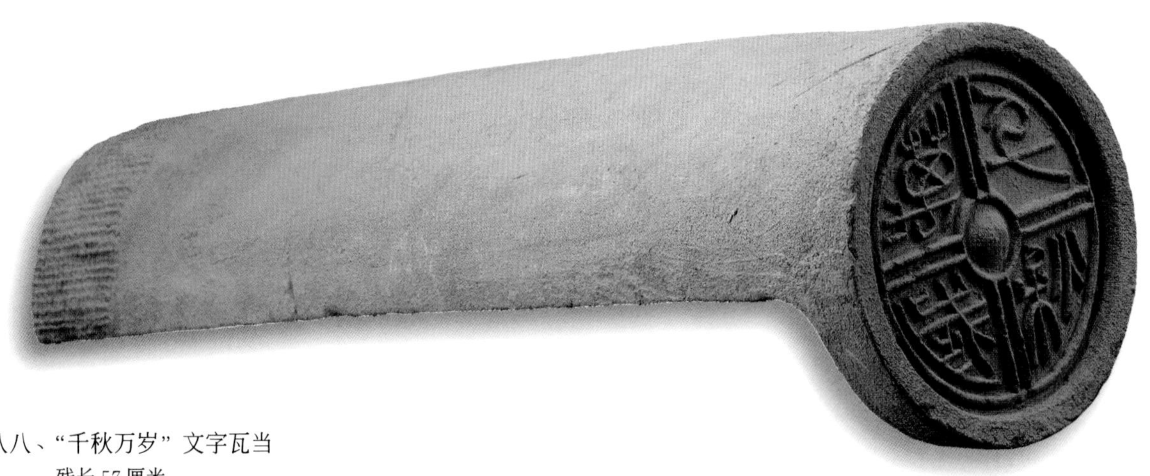

八八、"千秋万岁" 文字瓦当
残长57厘米，
瓦当面径18厘米。
帝陵南阙门遗址出土
"Everlasting eaves tile"
Length (damaged): 57cm,
diameter: 18cm
Unearthed at the ruins of the South Gate

八九、“与天无极”文字瓦当

面径 16 厘米。

帝陵南阙门遗址出土

"Timeless eaves tile"

Diameter: 16cm

Unearthed at the ruins of the South Gate

九〇、带瓦当筒瓦

长 48 厘米，

瓦当面径 17.3 厘米。

当面文字：“长生无极”。

“罗经石”遗址出土

Semi tube-shaped tile with an eaves tile

Length (damaged): 48cm,

diameter: 17.3cm

Unearthed at the ruins of the South Gate

九一、“与天久长” 文字瓦当
面径 17 厘米。
帝陵南阙门遗址出土
"Long lasting eaves tile"
Diameter: 17cm
Unearthed at the ruins of the South Gate

九二、“长乐未央” 文字瓦当
面径 20.6 厘米。
帝陵南阙门遗址出土
"Eternal happiness eaves tile"
Diameter:20.6cm
Unearthed at the ruins of the South Gate

九三、"永奉无疆" 文字瓦当

直径17.5厘米。

帝陵南阙门遗址出土

"Longevity eaves tile"

Diameter: 17.5cm

Unearthed at the ruins of the South Gate

九四、云纹瓦当

直径15.2厘米。

帝陵南阙门遗址出土

An eaves tile with cloud pattern

Diameter: 15.2cm

Unearthed at the ruins of the South Gate

九五、云纹瓦当
直径16.7厘米。
帝陵南阙门遗址出土
A eaves tile with cloud pattern
Diameter: 16.7cm
Unearthed at the ruins of the South Gate

九六、红色草拌泥墙皮
帝陵南阙门遗址出土
Red wall coating of mixed grass and mud
Unearthed at the ruins of the South Gate

九七、陶脊兽

残长 19,

高 14 厘米。

帝陵南阙门遗址出土

Animal shaped ornament on the ridge of a Palace

Length: 19cm,

height:14cm

Unearthed at the ruins of the South Gate

九八、回纹铺地方砖
边长34.5厘米。
帝陵南阙门遗址出土
Square brick with meander patterns
Length: 34.5cm
Unearthed at the ruins of the South Gate

九九、青龙纹空心砖
残长53厘米，
宽35厘米。
“罗经石”遗址出土
Hollow brick with Green Dragon design
Length (damaged):53cm
width:35cm
Unearthed from the ruins of the pelorus

一〇〇、玄武（龟蛇缠绕）纹空心砖
残长52厘米，
宽34厘米。
“罗经石”遗址出土
Hollow brick with Sombre Warrior design
Length (damaged):52cm,
width:34cm
Unearthed from the ruins of the pelorus

一〇一、“长乐未央”文字瓦当
面径16.5厘米。
“罗经石”遗址出土
"Eternal happiness eaves tile"
Diameter:16.5cm
Unearthed from the ruins of the pelorus

一〇二、云纹瓦当

面径15.5厘米。

帝陵南阙门遗址出土

An eaves tile with cloud pattern

Diameter: 15.5cm

Unearthed from the ruins of the pelorus

一〇三、云纹瓦当
面径16.5厘米。
“罗经石”遗址出土
An eaves tile with cloud pattern
Diameter: 16.5cm
Unearthed from the ruins of the pelorus

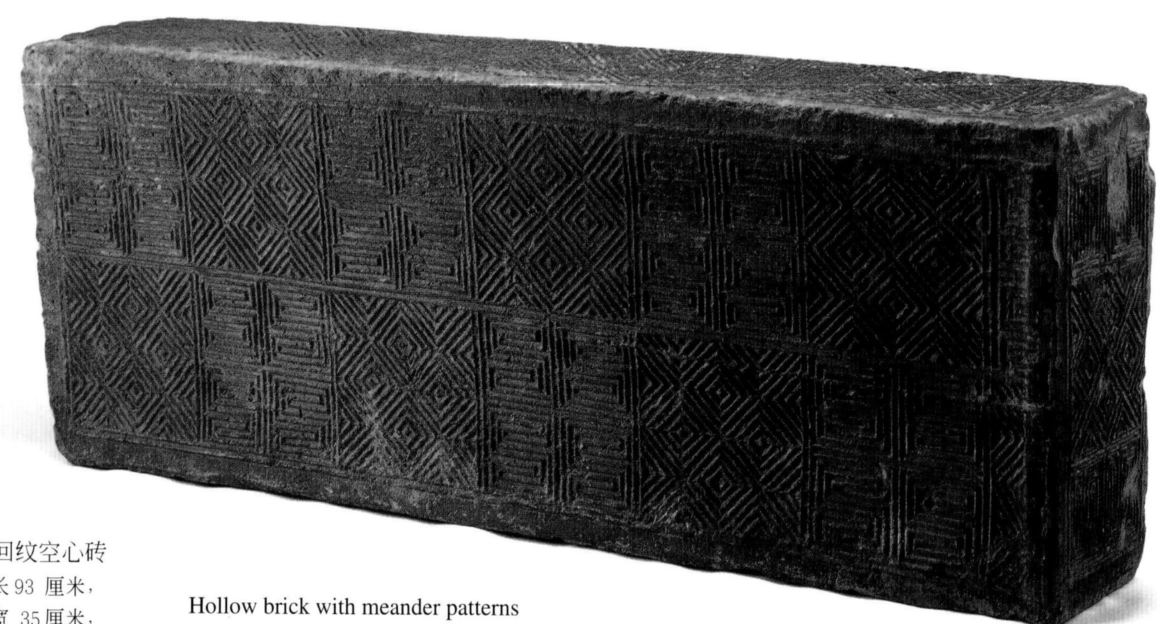

一〇四、回纹空心砖
长93 厘米，
宽 35厘米，
厚16.5 厘米。
阳陵邑遗址出土
Hollow brick with meander patterns
Length:93cm,
width:35cm
Unearthed from the ruins of the county seat of Yangling

一〇五、铁釜

高19.3厘米，
腹径23.6厘米。
南区从葬坑出土

An iron pot

Height: 19.3cm,
diameter: 23.6cm
Unearthed in the southern area of the burial pits

一〇六、陶釜、甑、灶
灶长38厘米，
南区从葬坑出土
Pottery pot, steamer, and cooking stove
Length of the stove: 38cm
Unearthed in the southern area of the burial pits

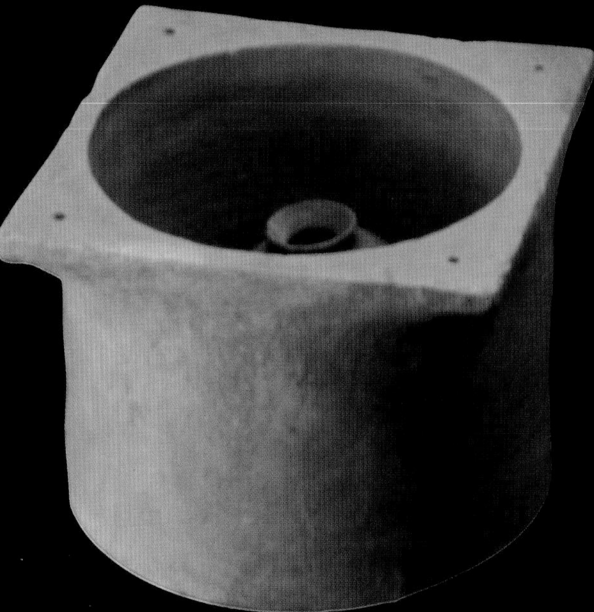

一〇七、陶井
高16 厘米，
直径18.2 厘米。
南区从葬坑出土
A pottery well
Height: 16cm
diameter: 18.2cm
Unearthed in the southern area of the burial pits

一〇八、盛有粮食的陶罐
高 13 厘米，
腹径 16 厘米。
陪葬墓园出土
A pottery jar containing grain
Height: 13cm
diameter: 16cm
Unearthed from the accompanying burial ground

一〇九、陶仓底部堆塑的胡人头像

陪葬墓园出土

Pottery ornament of a human head on the storage

Unearthed from the accompanying burial ground

一一〇、圆筒形陶仓
高 40 厘米，
腹径26.5厘米。
陪葬墓园出土
Pottery storage
Height: 40cm,
diameter: 26.5cm
Unearthed from the accompanying burial ground

一一一、房屋形陶仓 A
长 55.5 厘米、
宽 33 厘米、
高 50 厘米、
陪葬墓园出土
House-designed pottery storage A
Length: 55.5cm
width: 33cm
height: 50cm
Unearthed from the accompanying burial ground

一一二、房屋形陶仓 B
长 31 厘米，
宽 18 厘米，
高 24.8 厘米。
陪葬墓园出土
House-designed pottery storage B
Length: 31cm,
width: 18cm,
height: 24.8cm
Unearthed from the accompanying burial ground

一一三、素面带盖陶仓
高 47.5 厘米、
边长 25 厘米。
陪葬墓园出土
Undecorated pottery storage with lid
Height: 47.5cm,
length: 25cm
Unearthed from the accompanying burial ground

一一四、圆筒形带盖彩绘陶仓

高26.5厘米，

腹径15厘米。

陪葬墓园出土

Painted pottery storage with lid

Height:26.5cm,

diameter: 15cm

Unearthed from the accompanying burial ground

一一五、茧形陶壶
高 33 厘米，
最大腹径 36 厘米。
陪葬墓园出土
A cocoon shaped pottery pot
Height:33cm,
diameter: 38cm
Unearthed from the accompanying burial ground

一一七、彩绘陶壶

高 21.7 厘米。

陪葬墓园出土

A painted pottery pot

Height: 21.7cm

Unearthed from the accompanying burial ground

一一六、彩绘陶钫

高 37.5 厘米。

陪葬墓园出土

A painted square pottery pot

Height: 37.5cm

Unearthed from the accompanying burial ground

一一八、“般邑家”铜钫
高31.7厘米。
陪葬墓园出土
A square pot belonging to the House of Ban
Height: 31.7cm
Unearthed from the accompanying burial ground

一一九、般邑家铜锺

高 43.7 厘米，
口径 6.2 厘米，
腹径 34 厘米。
陪葬墓园出土

The bronze (Zhong) jar of "Banyijia"
Height: 43.7cm
Diameter of the mouth:6.2cm
Diameter of the belly:34cm
Unearthed from the accompanying burial ground

般邑家铜锺肩部的铭文
内容为："般邑家铜锺
容十斗
第二
家工造

The inscription on the shoulder of the jar Contents:

The bronze(Zhong)jar of "Banyijia"
Volume:10dou
Weight:35jin
This jar was the second of its kind
The jar was made in the workshop owaed by the noble of "Ban".

一二一、釉陶壶
高36.5厘米。
陪葬墓园出土
A glazed pottery pot
Height: 36.5cm
Unearthed from the accompanying burial ground

一二二、彩绘陶鼎
高14.5厘米。
陪葬墓园出土
A painted pottery ding
Height: 14.5cm
Unearthed from the accompanying burial ground

一二三、彩绘陶盆
径38.4厘米。
陪葬墓园出土
A painted pottery basin
Diameter: 38.4cm
Unearthed from the accompanying burial ground

一二四、陶盆底部的彩绘纹饰
he colorful decorative patterns
on the bottom of the basin

一二五、陶魁
长20厘米。
陪葬墓园出土
A pottery ladle
Length: 20cm
Unearthed from the accompanying burial ground

一二六、陶鱼
长16.2厘米。
陪葬墓园出土
A pottery fish
Length: 16. 2cm
Unearthed from the accompanying burial ground

一二七、陶炉及釜、甑、钵
高 38.6 厘米。
陪葬墓园出土
Pottery stove, steamer, and bowl
Height: 38.6cm
Unearthed from the accompanying burial ground

一二八、陶灶、陶甑灶
长24厘米。
陪葬墓园出土
Pottery stove and steamer
Length: 24cm
Unearthed from the accompanying burial ground

一二九、陶灶上的图案
Decorative patterns on the pottery stove

一三〇、铜盆
口径9厘米。
帝陵东侧从葬坑出土
A copper basin
Bore: 9cm
Unearthed from the eastern
side of the Emperor's tomb

一三一、铜钵

口径25厘米。

帝陵东侧从葬坑出土

A brass bowl

Bore: 25cm

Unearthed from the eastern side of the Emperor's tomb

一三二、铜鍪

口径3.5厘米。

帝陵东侧从葬坑出土

A copper pot

Bore: 3.5cm

Unearthed from the eastern side of the Emperor's tomb

一三三、铜甗 ►

高14.1厘米。

陪葬墓园出土

A copper yan (pot and steamer put together)

Height: 14.1cm

Unearthed from the accompanying burial ground

一三五、铜盆
口径26.6厘米。
陪葬墓园出土
A copper basin
Bore: 26.6cm
Unearthed from the accompanying burial ground

一三四、铜盆上的铺首衔环
An animal head holding a ring in the mouth on the copper basin

一三六、彩绘陶盆

口径14.5厘米，
高7.2厘米。
陪葬墓园出土

A painted pottery

Bore: 14.5cm

Unearthed from the accompanying burial ground

一三七、铜灯

通高7.2厘米。

陪葬墓园出土

A brass lamp

Height: 7.2cm

Unearthed from the accompanying burial ground

一三八、铜盆

高10.2厘米。

陪葬墓园出土

A copper basin

Height: 10.2cm

Unearthed from the accompanying burial ground

一三九、铜匜

通长37.4厘米

陪葬墓园出土

A copper yi (shallow oval ewer with spout and handle)

Length: 37.4cm

Unearthed from the accompanying burial ground

一四〇、铜豆

高 11.3 厘米。

陪葬墓园出土

Copper dou-a measurement of volume

Height: 11.3cm

Unearthed from the accompanying burial ground

一四一、铜豆上的兽首衔环
An animal head holding a ring in the mouth on the copper dou

一四二、铜熏炉

高 15.4 厘米。

陪葬墓园出土

A copper incense burner

Height: 15.4cm

Unearthed from the accompanying burial ground

一四三、铁染器

长32厘米。

陪葬墓园出土

An iron charcoal stove

Length: 32cm

Unearthed from the accompanying burial ground

一四四、铜鍪

高6.6厘米。

南区从葬坑出土

A copper pot

Height: 6.6cm

Unearthed from the accompanying burial ground

一四五、铜鍪
口径6.1厘米。
南区从葬坑出土
A copper pot
Bore: 6.1cm
Unearthed from the accompanying burial ground

一四六、铜带钩
长4.3厘米。
南区从葬坑出土
A copper belt hook
Length: 4.3cm
Unearthed from the accompanying burial ground

一四七、铜带钩一组
南区从葬坑出土
A set of copper belt hooks
Unearthed in the southern area of the burial pits

一四八、铜带钩一组
长9.3、11.4、12.4厘米。
陪葬墓园出土
A set of copper belt hooks
Length: 9.3cm, 11.4cm, 12.4cm
Unearthed from the accompanying burial ground

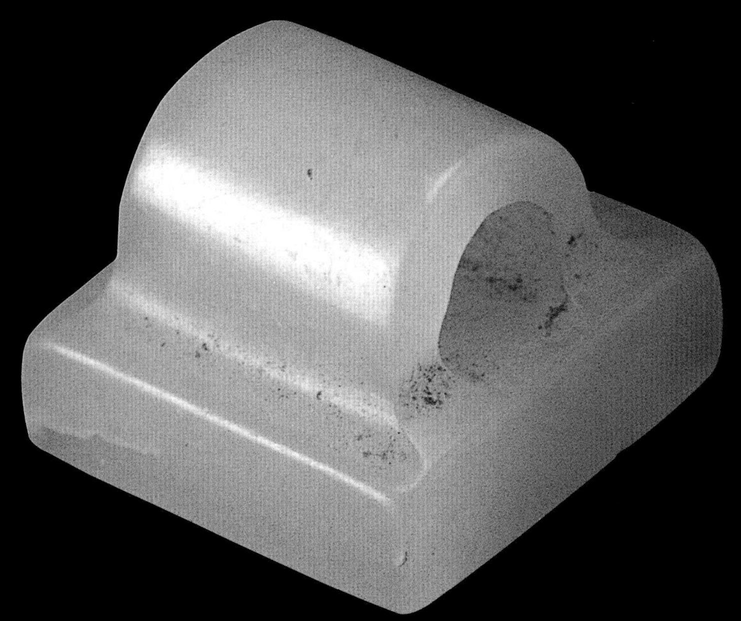

一四九、玉印坯
边长1.4厘米，
高1.1厘米。
陪葬墓园出土
A jade seal base
Length: 1.4cm, height: 1.1cm
Unearthed from the accompanying burial ground

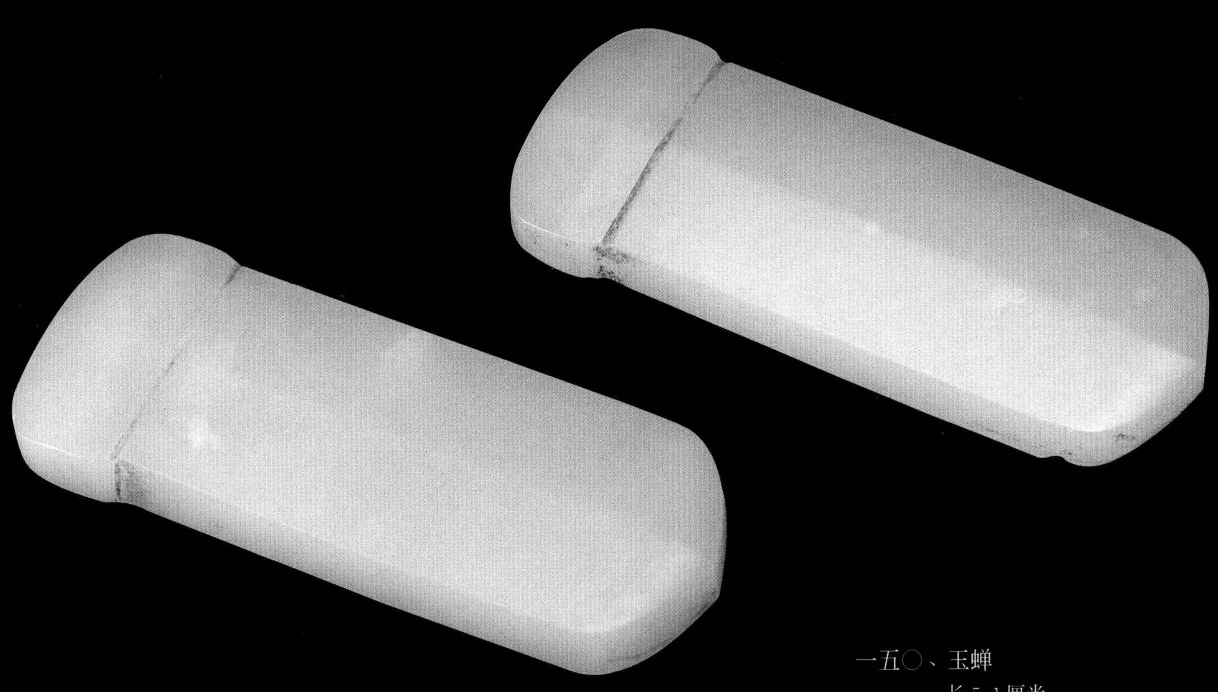

一五〇、玉蝉
长5.1厘米。
陪葬墓园出土
Jade cicadas
Length: 5.1cm
Unearthed from the accompanying burial ground

一五一、玉蝉

长5.0厘米。

陪葬墓园出土

A jade cicada

Length: 5cm

Unearthed from the accompanying burial ground

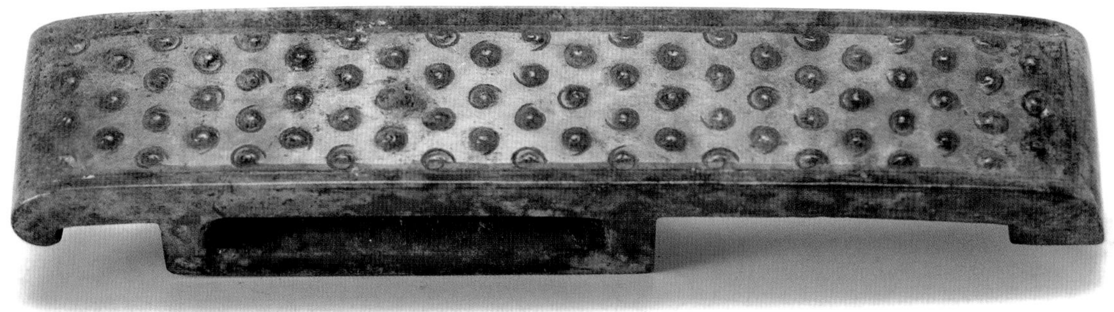

一五二、玉剑璏

长9.4厘米，

宽1.9厘米。

陪葬墓园出土

A jade sword tube

Length: 9.4cm

width:1.9cm

Unearthed from the accompanying burial ground

一五三、重圈昭明镜

直径10.7厘米。

陪葬墓园出土

A brass mirror with double-ring patterns

Diameter: 10.7cm

Unearthed from the accompanying burial ground

一五四、连弧铭带镜

直径 13.5 厘米。

镜背文字为“内清质以昭而明光而象夫日月心而忽而忠而不泄。”

陪葬墓园出土

A brass mirror

Diameter: 13.5cm

Unearthed from the accompanying burial ground

一五五、四乳蟠螭镜

直径 16.4 厘米。

陪葬墓园出土

A brass mirror of four nipples and interlaced hydra design

Diameter: 16.4cm

Unearthed from the accompanying burial ground

一五六、四乳神兽镜

直径18.6厘米。

陪葬墓园出土

A brass mirror of four-nipples and mythical animal design

Diameter: 18.6cm

Unearthed from the accompanying burial ground

一五七、四乳四虺镜

直径16.4厘米。

陪葬墓园出土

A brass mirror of coiled serpentdesign

Diameter: 16.4cm

Unearthed from the accompanying burial ground

一五八、花瓣蟠螭镜

直径 13.4 厘米。

陪葬墓园出土

A brass mirror of flower and interlaced hydra design

Diameter: 13.4cm

Unearthed from the accompanying burial ground

一五九、草叶铭文镜

直径 9.7 厘米。

镜背文字: “君来何伤慎毋相忘”

陪葬墓园出土

A brass mirror of leaf design with inscriptions

Diameter: 9.7cm

Unearthed from the accompanying burial ground

一六〇、乳丁博局镜

直径21.2厘米。

陪葬墓园出土

A brass mirror with chessboard design

Diameter: 21.2cm

Unearthed from the accompanying burial ground

一六一、玉璧
外径9.2厘米。
帝陵东侧从葬坑出土
Jade bi (burial objects)
Diameter: 9.2cm
Unearthed from the eastern side of the Emperor's tomb

一六二、鸟形铜籥
长5.9厘米。
陪葬墓园出土
Bird designed ornament on weapons
Length: 5.9cm
Unearthed from the accompanying burial ground

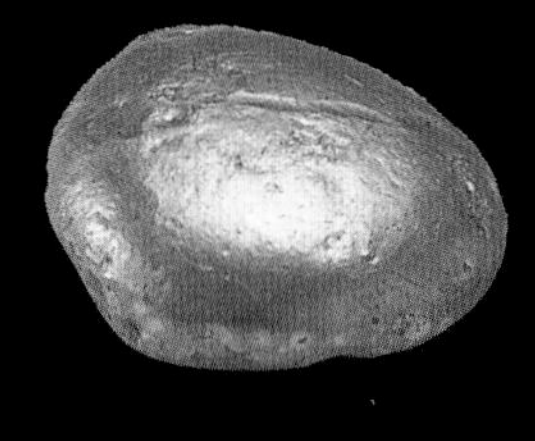
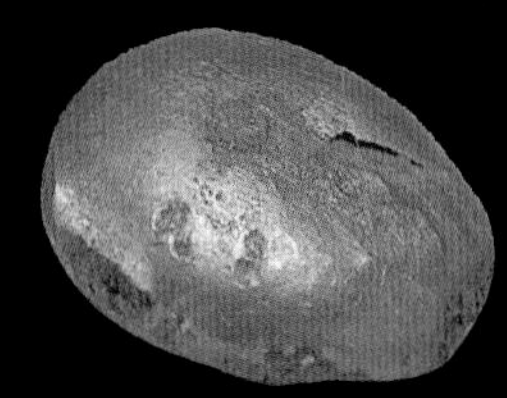
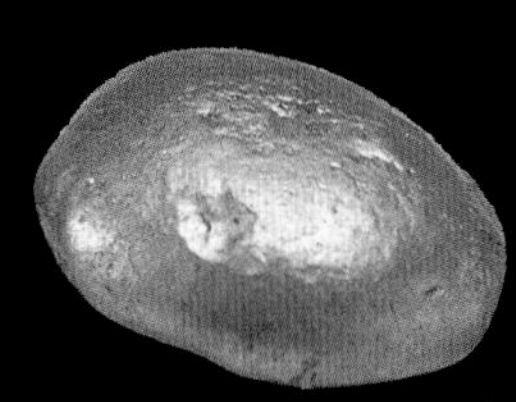
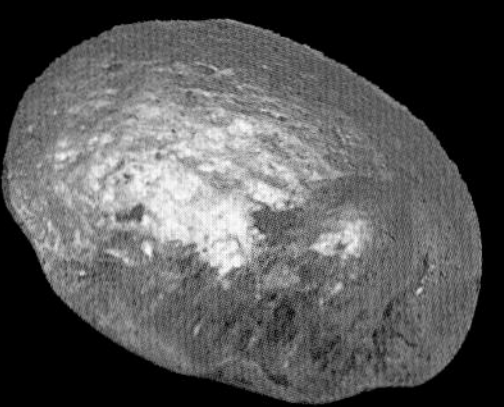

一六三、金饼一组
直径1.4厘米。
南区从葬坑出土
A set of gold plates
Diameter: 1.4cm
Unearthed in the southern area of the bu

一六四、"半两" 铜钱一组
直径2.4厘米。
南区从葬坑出土
A group of half-liang copper coins
Diameter: 2.4cm
Unearthed in the southern area of the burial pits

一六五、"太官之印" 铜印章
帝陵东侧第 16 号从葬坑出土
Copper seal bearing the inscriptions "tai-guan"-an imperial official Unearthed from the eastern side of the Emperor's tomb

一六六、"周应" 铜印章
陪葬墓园出土
A copper seal belonging to Zhouyin

一六七、铜斗

径11.3厘米，
高8.7厘米。
南区从葬坑出土

A copper dou (a measurement of volume)

Bore: 11.3cm,
height: 8.7cm
Unearthed in the southern area of the burial pits

一六九、铜量器

径2.9、2.5厘米，

长10.2、9.4厘米。

南区从葬坑出土

Copper volume

Bore: 2.9、2.5,

Length: 10.2cm, 9.4cm

Unearthed in the southern area of the burial pits

一六八、铜升一组

径5.9、4.7、4.2、2.8厘米，

高3.4、2.7、2.4、1.6厘米。

南区从葬坑出土

A set of copper sheng (a measurement of volume)

Bore: 5.9cm, 4.7cm, 4.2cm, 2.8cm,

height: 3.4cm, 2.7cm, 2.4cm, 1.6cm

Unearthed in the southern area of the burial pits

一七〇、铜累一组
径4.7-1.9厘米,
高3.2-1.2厘米。
南区从葬坑出土
A set of copper lei-sliding weight of steelyard
Diameter: 4.7-1.9cm,
height: 3.2-1.2cm
Unearthed in the southern area of the burial pits

一七一、铜累器一组
径 2.9-1.3厘米,
高1.7-0.7厘米。
南区从葬坑出土
A set of copper quan-sliding weight of steelyard
Diameter:2.9-1.3cm,
height: 1.7-0.7cm
Unearthed in the southern area of the burial pits

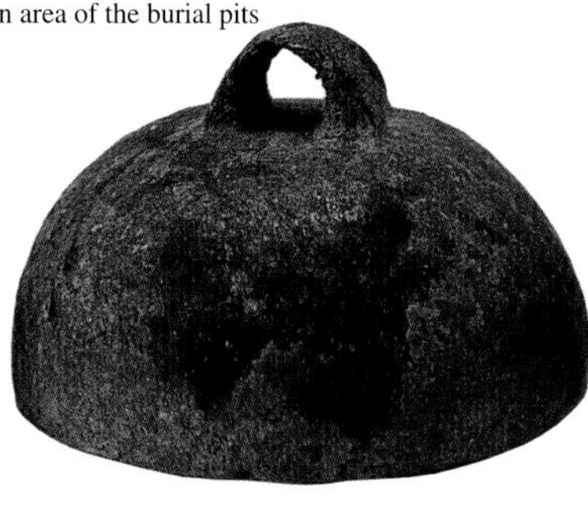

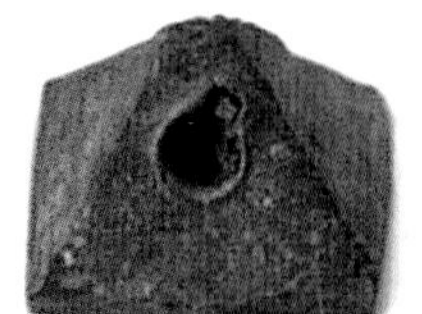
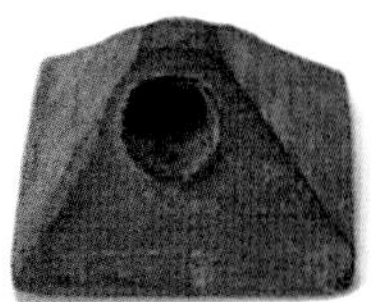

一七二、铜砝码一组

边长0.7厘米，
高0.5厘米。
南区从葬坑出土

A set of copper weight

Length: 0.7cm,
height: 0.5cm
Unearthed in the southern area of the burial pits

一七三、铁累一组

径2.9、5.3、8厘米，
高1.7、3.2、5厘米。
南区从葬坑出土

A set of iron lei-sliding weight of steelyard

Diameter: 2.9cm, 5.3cm, 8cm,
height: 1.7cm, 3.2cm, 5cm
Unearthed in the southern area of the burial pits

一七四、沉箭式陶漏壶

径10.1厘米，
高22.3厘米。
帝陵东侧从葬坑出土

Earthenware dripping pot for measuring time

Diameter: 10.1cm,
height: 22.3cm
Unearthed from the accompanying pits of the Emperor's tomb

一七五、铜弩机

长6.7厘米，

宽3.9厘米。

南区从葬坑出土

A copper archery device

Length: 6.7cm,

width: 3.9cm

Unearthed in the southern area of the burial pits

一七六、铜弩机

长5.9厘米，

宽2.7厘米。

陪葬墓园出土

A copper archery device

Length: 5.9cm,

width: 2.7cm

Unearthed from the accompanying burial ground

一七七、铜镞一组

长3—3.4厘米。

南区从葬坑出土

A bunch of copper arrow-heads

Length: 3-3.4cm,

Unearthed in the southern area of the burial pits

一七八、铜镞及其木梃遗迹

镞长3.1厘米。

陪葬墓园出土

Traces of copper area-heads and the wooden ends

Length of the ends: 3.1cm

Unearthed from the accompanying burial ground

一七九、铁四棱矛头
长3.8厘米。
南区从葬坑出土
Four-edged iron spears
Length: 3.8cm
Unearthed in the southern area
of the burial pits

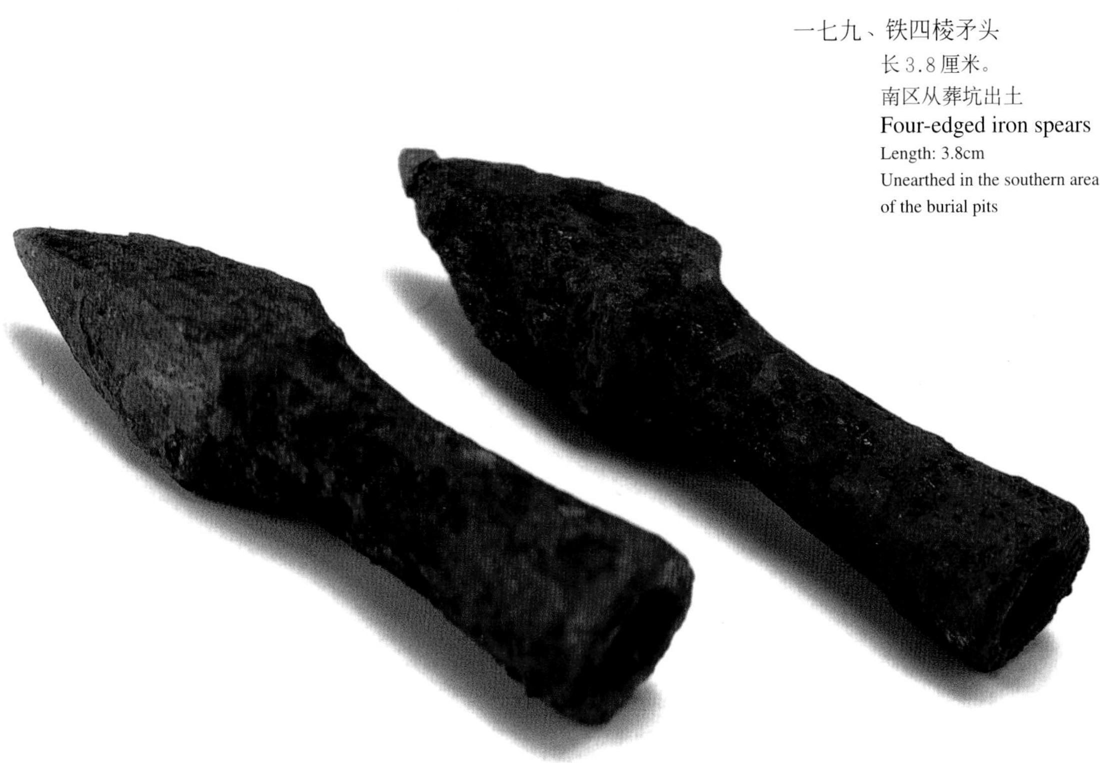

一八〇、铜戈
长24.7厘米。
陪葬墓园出土
A copper hook weapon
Length 24.7cm
Unearthed from the accompanying burial ground

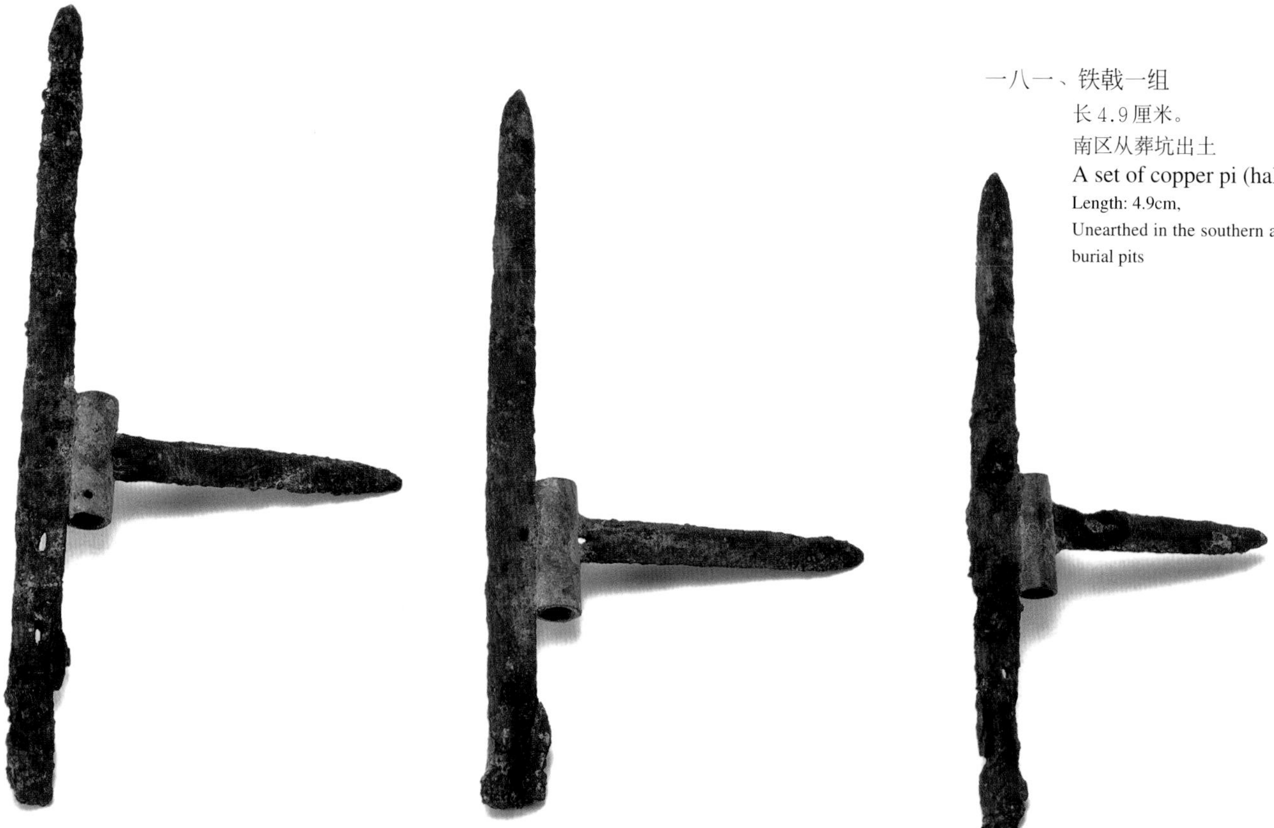

一八一、铁戟一组
长4.9厘米。
南区从葬坑出土
A set of copper pi (halberd)
Length: 4.9cm,
Unearthed in the southern area of th burial pits

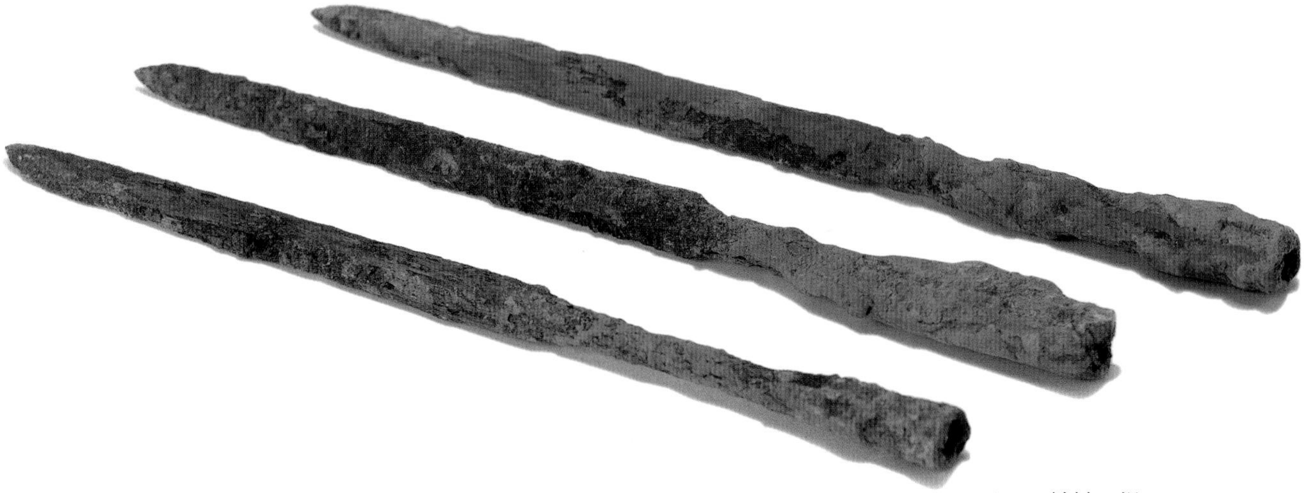

一八二、铁铍一组

长 17.2 厘米。

南区从葬坑出土

A set of iron pi (long spear)

Length:17.2cm,

Unearthed in the southern area of the burial pits

一八三、铁剑一组

长 37.6、36.2、34.4 厘米。

南区从葬坑出土

A set of iron swords

Length: 37.6cm, 36.2cm, 34.4cm

Unearthed in the southern area of the burial pits

一八四、剑鞘遗迹

南区从葬坑出土

Traces of scabbards

Unearthed in the southern area of the burial pits

一八五、铜剑

长42.3厘米。

陪葬墓园出土

A copper sword

Length: 42.3cm

Unearthed from the accompanying burial ground

一八六、铜墩一组

径1.0厘米,

高2.0厘米。

南区从葬坑出土

A set of copper weapon parts

Diameter: 1.0cm, height: 2.0cm

Unearthed in the southern area of the burial pits

一八七、铜车軎

长4.0 厘米，
径2.8厘米。
南区从葬坑出土
Copper wei (axle endpiece)
Length: 4.0cm, diameter: 2.8cm
Unearthed in the southern area of the burial pits

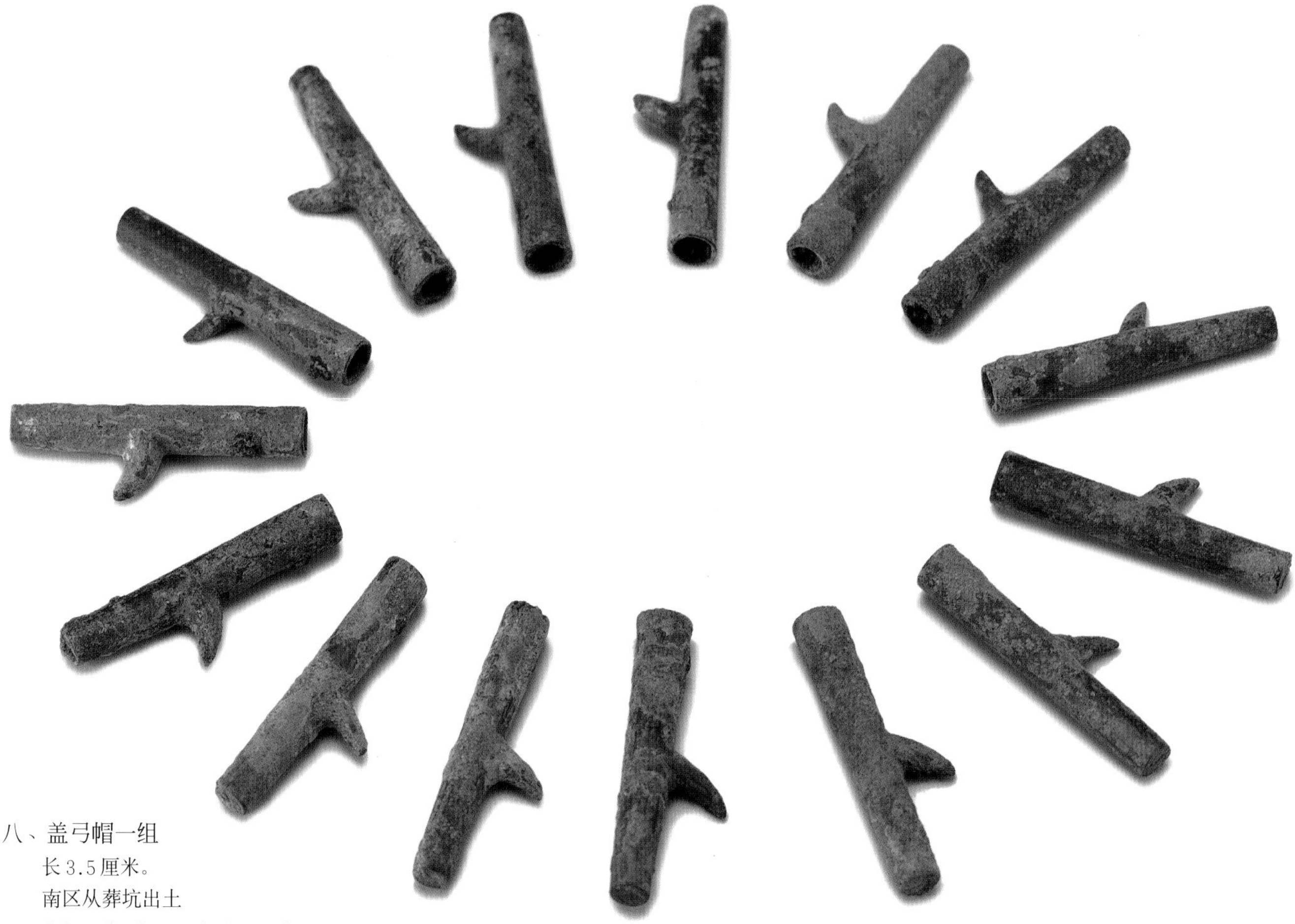

一八八、盖弓帽一组

长3.5厘米。
南区从葬坑出土
A bunch of canopied caps for sheathing the bows
Length: 3.5cm
Unearthed in the southern area of the burial pits

▼ 一八九、铜俾倪

长 10.5 厘米，

径 1.7 厘米。

南区从葬坑出土

A copper bi-ni (connecting the chamber and the canopy of a chariot)

Length: 10.5cm,

diameter:1.7cm

Unearthed in the southern area of the burial pits

一九〇、铜衔、铁镳
衔长8.5厘米，
镳长8.2厘米。
南区从葬坑出土
Copper xian (curb bit), biao (curb chain)
Length of xian: 8.5cm,
biao: 8.2cm
Unearthed in the southern area of the burial pits

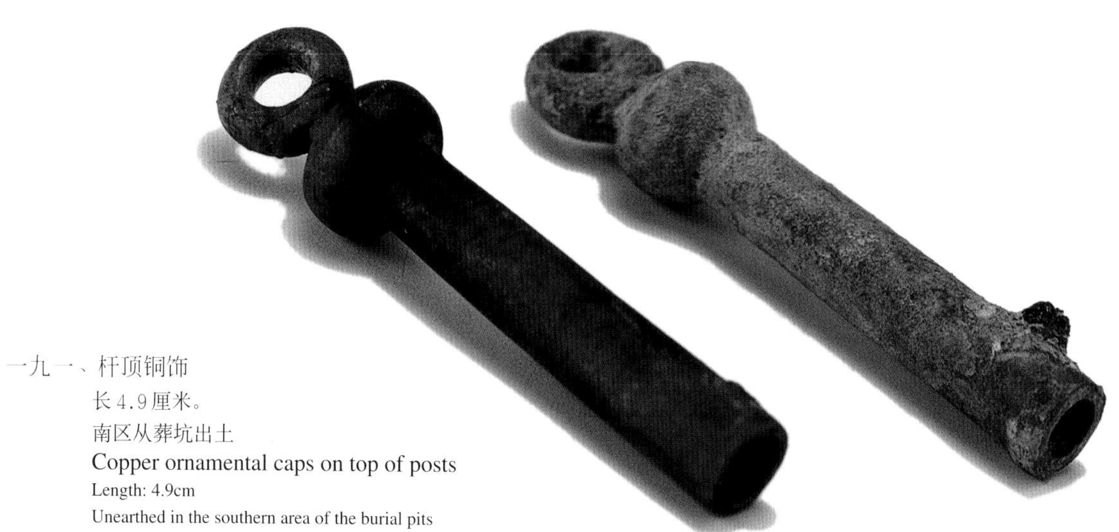

一九一、杆顶铜饰
长4.9厘米。
南区从葬坑出土
Copper ornamental caps on top of posts
Length: 4.9cm
Unearthed in the southern area of the burial pits

一九二、铜承弓器
长7.4厘米。
南区从葬坑出土
Copper crotches for crossbow
Length: 7.4cm
Unearthed in the southern area of the burial pits

一九三、鎏金铜衡末一组
径1.3厘米，
高2.3厘米。
陪葬墓园出土
A set of gold-plated copper chariot components
Diameter: 1.3cm,
height: 2.3cm
Unearthed from the accompanying burial ground

一九四、鎏金铜车軜
长3.1厘米，
宽1.4厘米。
陪葬墓园出土
Gold-plated connecting devices of chariots
Length: 3.1cm,
width: 1.4cm
Unearthed from the accompanying burial ground

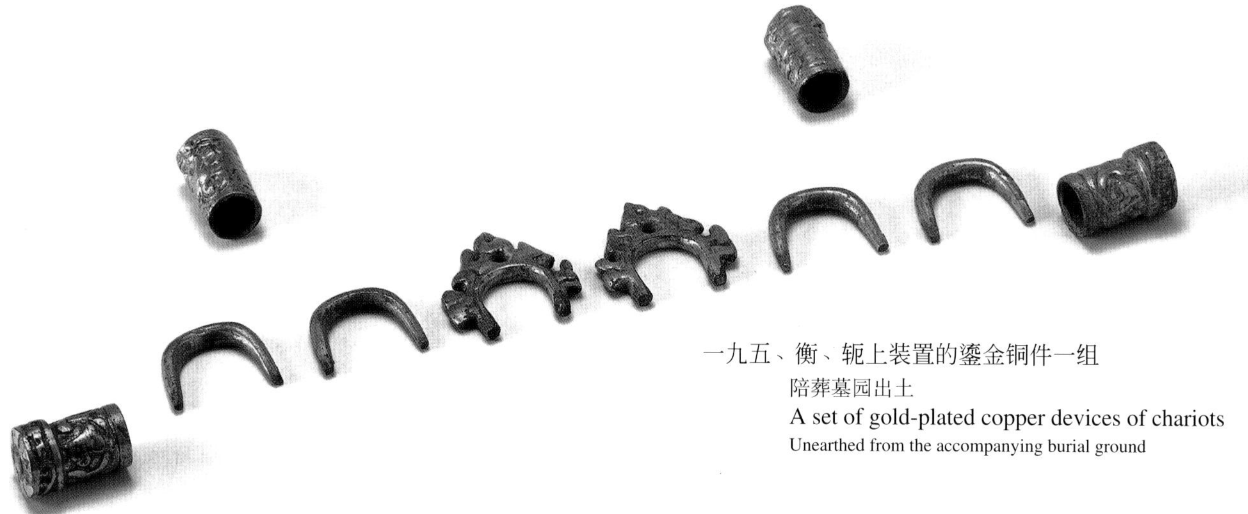

一九五、衡、轭上装置的鎏金铜件一组
陪葬墓园出土
A set of gold-plated copper devices of chariots
Unearthed from the accompanying burial ground

一九六、鎏金铜车饰
高1.6厘米，
径1.7厘米。
陪葬墓园出土
Gold-plated copper ornaments for chariot
Height: 1.6cm,
diameter: 1.7cm
Unearthed from the accompanying burial ground

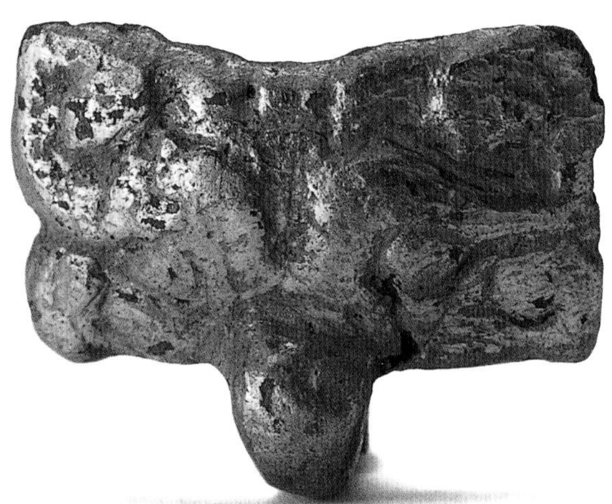

一九七、鎏金铜铺首
长1.8厘米，
宽1.3厘米。
陪葬墓园出土
A gold-plated copper ornament of an animal head
Length: 1.8cm,
width: 1.3cm
Unearthed from the accompanying burial ground

一九八、鎏金铜车构件
长3.1厘米，
宽4.5厘米。
陪葬墓园出土
Gold-plated copper devices of chariots
Length: 3.18cm,
width: 4.5cm
Unearthed from the accompanying burial ground

一九九、鎏金铜承弓器
长5.4厘米。
陪葬墓园出土
Gold-plated copper crotches for crossbow
Length: 5.4cm
Unearthed from the accompanying burial ground

二〇〇、鎏金铜车軎
长2.1厘米，
径1－2厘米。
陪葬墓园出土
Gold-plated copper wei (axle endpiece)
Length: 2.1cm,
diameter: 1 - 2cm
Unearthed from the accompanying burial ground

二〇一、鎏金虎头形铜车饰
长2.8厘米，
宽2.1厘米。
陪葬墓园出土
Gold-plated copper ornaments of tiger heads on chariots
Length: 2.8cm,
width: 2.1cm
Unearthed from the accompanying burial ground

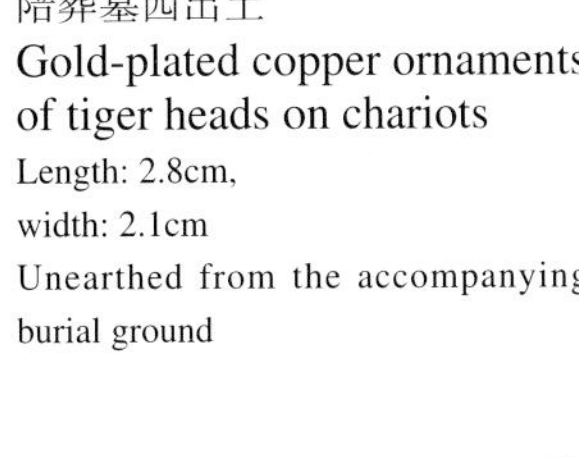

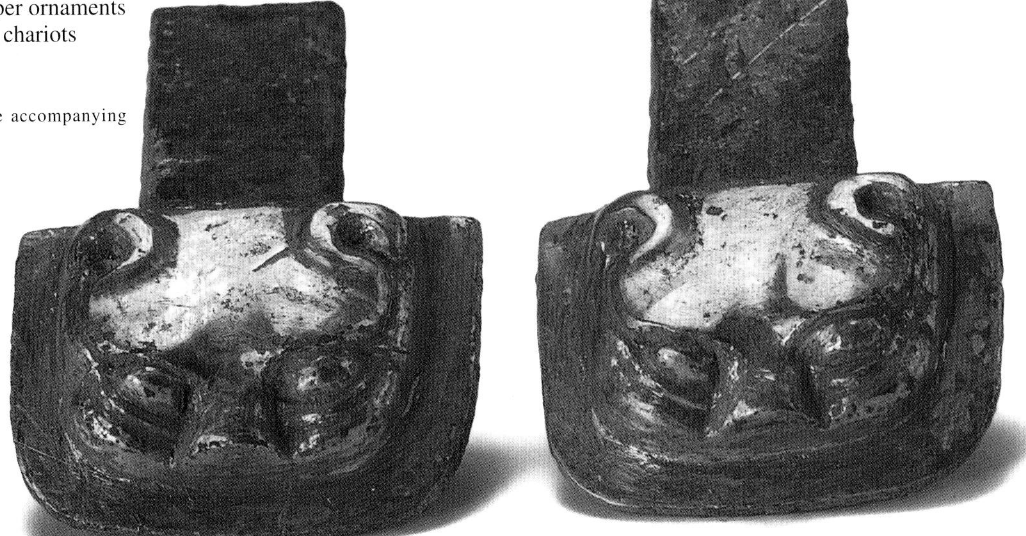

二〇二、铜銮铃
高4.2、3.5厘米，
口径3.0、3.5厘米。
陪葬墓园出土
Copper bells
Height: 4.2cm, 3.5cm,
diameter: 3.0cm, 3.5cm
Unearthed from the accompanying burial ground

二〇三、衔、镳
长11.3、11.7厘米。
陪葬墓园出土
A curb bit and a curb chain
Length: 11.3cm, 11.7cm
Unearthed from the accompanying burial ground

二〇四、鎏金铜节约一组
长0.9—1.4厘米。
陪葬墓园出土
Gold-plated copper devices for halter
Length: 0.9 - 1.4cm
Unearthed from the accompanying burial ground

二〇五、鎏金铜车饰
径4.1厘米。
陪葬墓园出土
Gold-plated copper ornaments on chariot
Diameter: 4.1cm
Unearthed from the accompanying burial ground

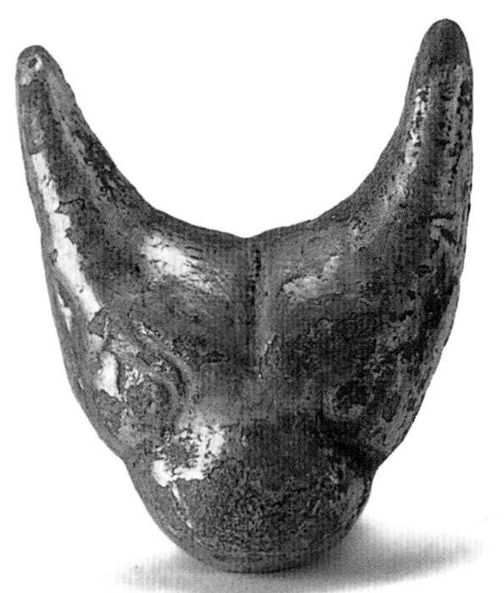

二〇六、鎏金铜车饰一组
高1.4厘米。
陪葬墓园出土
A set of gold-plated copper ornaments on chariot
Height: 1.4cm
Unearthed from the accompanying burial ground

二〇七、鎏金铜衔、镳
长7.8 厘米。
陪葬墓园出土
Gold-plated copper xian (curb bit), biao (curb chain)
Length: 7.8cm
Unearthed from the accompanying burial ground

二〇八、鎏金铜镳一组
长 7.2 厘米。
陪葬墓园出土
A set of gold-plated curb chains
Length: 7.2cm
Unearthed from the accompanying burial ground

二〇九、鎏金铜节约
径 1.2 厘米。
陪葬墓园出土
Gold-plated copper devices for halter
Diameter: 1.2cm
Unearthed from the accompanying burial ground

二一〇、鎏金铜盖弓帽一组
长3.6厘米。
陪葬墓园出土
A bunch of gold-plated canopied caps for sheathing the bows
Length: 3.6cm
Unearthed in the southern area of the burial pits

二一一、鎏金铜俾倪

长12厘米。

陪葬墓园出土

Gold-plated copper bini(connecting the chamber and the canopy of a chariot)

Length: 12cm

Unearthed in the southern area of the burial pits

二一二、铜带銙

长2.5厘米。

南区从葬坑出土

A copper belt hook

Length: 2.5cm

Unearthed in the southern area of the burial pits

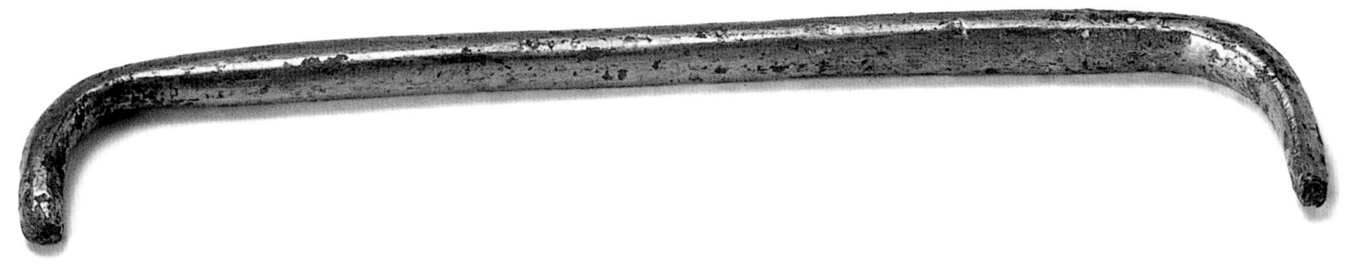

二一三、鎏金铜车构件
长3.1厘米。
陪葬墓园出土
A gold-plated copper device on chariot
Length: 3.1cm
Unearthed in the southern area of the burial pits

二一四、铜带扣
长0.9厘米，
宽0.7厘米。
陪葬墓园出土
Copper belt buckles
Length: 0.9cm,
width: 0.7cm
Unearthed in the southern
area of the burial pits

二一五、铜带扣
长1.6厘米，
宽1.3厘米。
陪葬墓园出土
A copper belt buckle
Length: 1.6cm,
width: 1.3cm
Unearthed in the southern area of the burial pits

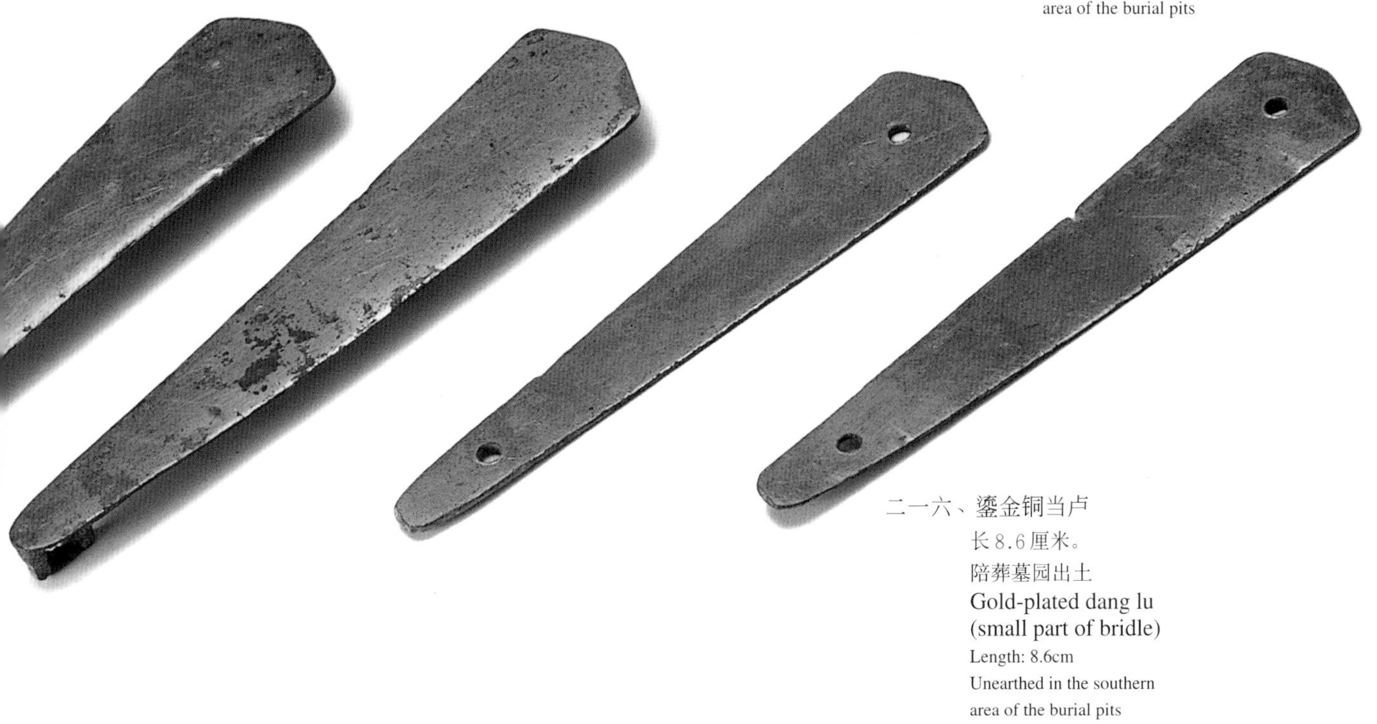

二一六、鎏金铜当卢
长8.6厘米。
陪葬墓园出土
Gold-plated dang lu (small part of bridle)
Length: 8.6cm
Unearthed in the southern area of the burial pits

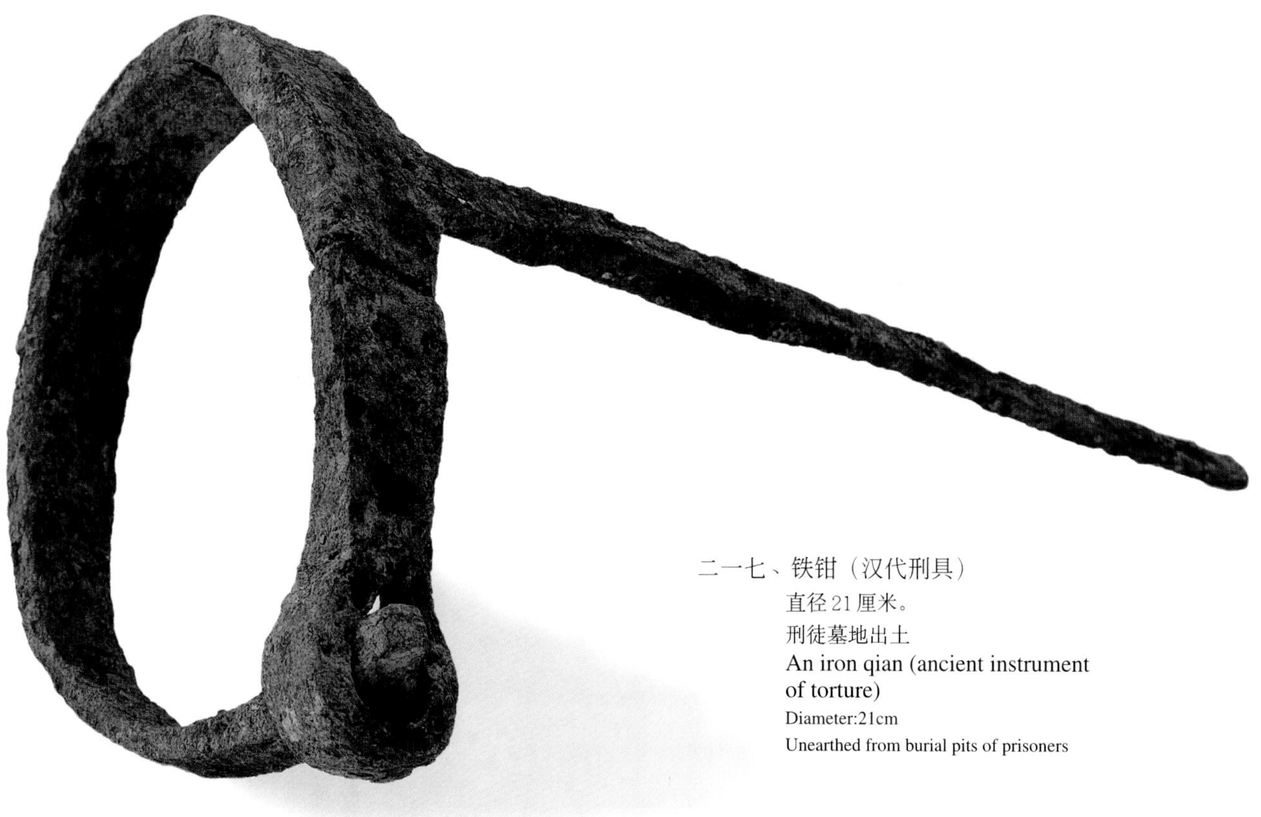

二一七、铁钳（汉代刑具）

直径21厘米。

刑徒墓地出土

An iron qian (ancient instrument of torture)

Diameter:21cm

Unearthed from burial pits of prisoners

二一八、铁钛

直径10.5厘米。

刑徒墓地出土

Iron shackles

Diameter: 10.5cm

Unearthed from burial pits of prisoners

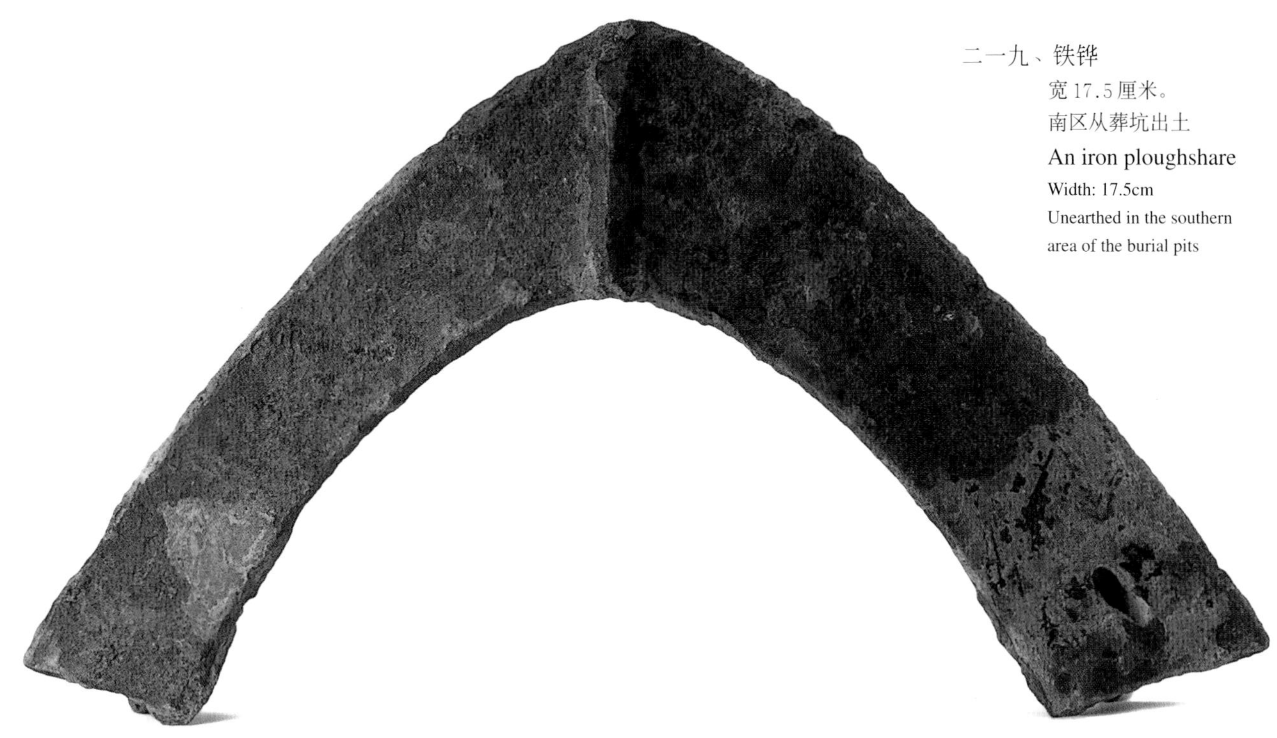

二一九、铁铧
宽17.5厘米。
南区从葬坑出土
An iron ploughshare
Width: 17.5cm
Unearthed in the southern area of the burial pits

二二〇、铁工具：（斧、凿、锯、锸）
斧长2.8、宽2.4；
凿长6.2、宽1.0；
锯长10、宽1.8；
锸长4.1、宽2.4厘米。
南区从葬坑出土
Iron tools (axe, chisel, saw, spade)
Length: 2.8cm (axe), 6.2cm (chisel), 10cm (saw), 4.1cm (spade) Width: 2.4cm (axe), 1.0cm (chisel), 1.8cm (saw), 2.4cm (spade)
Unearthed in the southern area of the burial pits

二二一、铁锸
宽18.5、17.1、13厘米。
南区从葬坑出土
Iron spades
Width: 18.5cm, 17.1cm, 13cm
Unearthed in the southern area of the burial pits

二二二、铁夯头
径7.5厘米，
高8厘米。
南阙门遗址出土
An iron rammer
Diameter: 7.5cm, height: 8cm
Unearthed at the ruins of the South Gate

二二三、双面人铜饰
宽 4.7厘米。
陪葬墓园出土
A copper ornament of a double-faced head
Width: 4.7cm
Unearthed in the southern area of the burial pits

二二四、鎏金虎头饰件一组
帝陵东侧从葬坑出土
A group of gold-plated tiger-head ornaments
Unearthed from the eastern side of the Emperor's tomb

二二五、鎏金虎头饰件

帝陵东侧从葬坑出土

Gold-plated tiger-head ornaments

Unearthed from the eastern side of the Emperor's tomb

二二六、盗洞中发现的铁釜

口径 14.5,

高 20 厘米。

帝陵东侧 16 号从葬坑出土

An iron pot found in a burglary hole

Bore: 14.5cm,

height: 20cm

Unearthed from No.16 burial pit on the eastern side of the Emperor's tomb

二二七、铁釜中放置的铜构件

长 12.5 厘米。

帝陵东侧 16 号从葬坑出土

Copper devices put in the iron pot (of No.226)

Length: 12.5cm

Unearthed from No.16 burial pit on the eastern side of the Emperor's tomb

二二八、铜构件上的彩绘纹样

Painted decorative patterns on the copper devices

二二九、铁釜中放置的铜构件

帝陵东侧 16 号从葬坑出土

Copper devices put in the iron pot (of No.226)

Unearthed from No.16 burial pit on the eastern side of the Emperor's tomb

二三〇、铜构件

长 4 厘米。

帝陵东侧从葬坑出土

A copper spare part

Length: 4cm

Unearthed from the eastern side of the Emperor's tomb

二三一、木箱上的铜铺首

长8.3厘米。

帝陵东侧从葬坑出土

A copper ornament of an animal head on wooden box

Length: 8.3cm

Unearthed from the eastern side of the Emperor's tomb

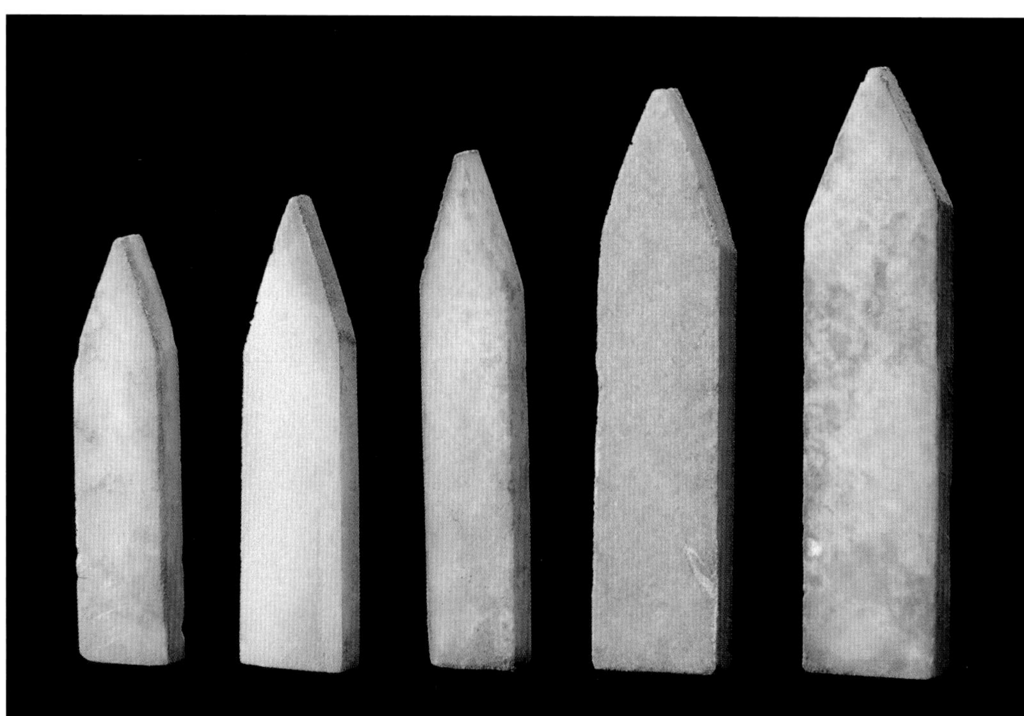

二三二、玉圭一组
长6.8-9.3厘米。
罗经石遗址出土
A set of jade gui (elongate
tablet as burial objects)
Length: 6.8 - 9.3cm
Unearthed from the ruins of t
pelorus

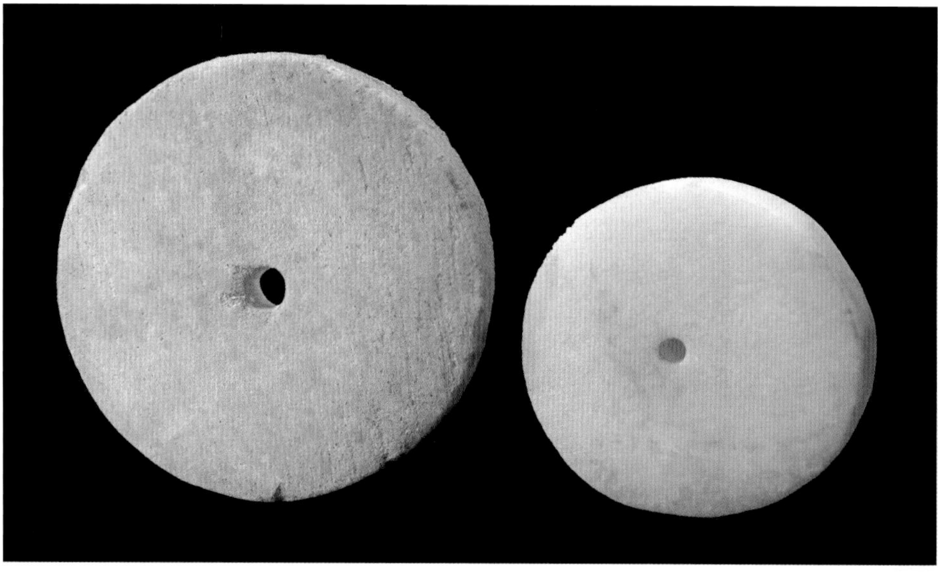

二三三、玉璧
直径3.7、4.8厘米。
"罗经石" 遗址出土
Jade pi (burial objects)
Diameter: 3.7cm, 4.8cm
Unearthed from the ruins of the pelorus

二三四、制俑模具
残长10厘米,
宽16厘米。
汉长安城出土
Mould for making potteries
Length: 10cm, width: 16cm
Unearthed in the ancient Han capital of Chang'an

二三五、陶质围棋盘
残长28厘米，
残宽18厘米。
帝陵南阙门遗址出土
Earthenware weiqi (go) chessboard
Length: 28cm,
width: 16cm
Unearthed at the ruins of the South Gate

二三六、六博盘
边长34.5厘米。
后陵陵园出土
Liubo plate-a sports game
Length: 34.5cm
Unearthed from the Empress's tomb

二三七、汉阳陵考古陈列馆外景

An outdoor scene of the Yangling Archaeological Exhibition Center

二三八、汉阳陵考古陈列馆展厅一角——陪葬墓园M 9 K 1 复原展示
A section of the exhibition hall in the Yangling Archaeological Exhibition Center-a replica of the burial pit M9K1

后记

阳陵的考古研究工作追根溯源，可以说是从二十世纪初开始的；但真正奠定基础、取得成效的是二十世纪七十至八十年代；二十世纪九十年代初阳陵南区从葬坑的发现和发掘则揭开了阳陵大规模发掘研究的序幕，具有十分重大的意义。时至新世纪，随着阳陵考古研究工作的逐步深入，汉景帝阳陵已成为举世瞩目的文物旅游景点，建成了面积巨大、景点众多，边发掘、边保护、边研究、边建设、边展示的“汉阳陵考古陈列馆”。追忆历史，展望未来，我们首先要感谢的是为阳陵考古研究工作披荆斩棘、开辟坦途的前辈考古学家，正是由于他们的辛勤耕耘和不懈努力，才有了阳陵考古工作硕果累累的今天和前程似锦的明天。

在阳陵多年的田野考古工作中，和我们朝夕相处、患难与共的有一大批能发掘、钻探，会制图、修复，多才多艺、任劳任怨的技工兄弟，没有他们一铲一铲地发掘，一张一张地绘图，一件一件地修复，我们这些所谓的“研究人员”必将一事无成。因此，我们要借此机会向他们道一声：“谢谢！你们辛苦了。”

阳陵的考古发掘、研究和文物保护工作得到了陕西省委、省政府、特别是陕西省文物局的正确领导；得到了西安文物保护中心、秦俑博物馆、西安市文物局、咸阳市文物局、咸阳市渭城区文物局等兄弟单位的无私援助；得到了高陵县、咸阳市渭城区等地各级领导的大力支持；得到了以咸阳市渭城区张家湾、后沟和高陵县梁村为代表的众多农民朋友的理解和协助；在此谨表谢意。

本图录的图片资料一部分是1990年至1994年的发掘成果，资料引用于1992年陕西旅游出版社出版的《中国阳陵彩俑》和2001年文物出版社出版的《汉阳陵考古陈列馆》等，大部分资料是1995年以来的发掘成果，特此说明。

由于时间紧张，加之水平有限，难免有错误之处，敬请专家和广大读者批评指正。

编者

2001年9月30日

图书在版编目（CIP）数据

汉阳陵/陕西省考古研究所编.—重庆：重庆出版社，2001.10
ISBN 7-5366-5403-0

Ⅰ.汉... Ⅱ.陕... Ⅲ.汉墓-发掘报告-咸阳市 Ⅳ.K878.85

中国版本图书馆CIP数据核字（2001）第051953号

陕西省考古研究所编
主编：焦南峰
副主编：王保平
执行编委：马永嬴、李岗
编委：肖健一、徐雍初、赵西晨、田书祯、丁文杉
图版摄影：王保平
英文翻译：张亚伦
日文翻译：小川能史

责任编辑：邹禾
装帧设计：邹禾、秦雪
封面题签：姚渝永
插图：邹禾
出版发行：重庆出版社
（重庆市长江二路205号）
制版印刷：深圳彩帝印刷实业有限公司
版次：2001年10月第一版第一次印刷
印数：1-3000册
开本：889 × 1194 1/16 印张：12
书号：ISBN 7-5366-5403-0/J · 875
定价：350圆（精装） 300圆（平装）